SpringerBriefs in Operations Research

SpringerBriefs present concise summaries of cutting-edge research and practical applications across a wide spectrum of fields. Featuring compact volumes of 50 to 125 pages, the series covers a range of content from professional to academic. Typical topics might include:

- A timely report of state-of-the art analytical techniques
- A bridge between new research results, as published in journal articles, and a contextual literature review
- A snapshot of a hot or emerging topic
- An in-depth case study or clinical example
- A presentation of core concepts that students must understand in order to make independent contributions

SpringerBriefs in Operations Research showcase emerging theory, empirical research, and practical application in the various areas of operations research, management science, and related fields, from a global author community. Briefs are characterized by fast, global electronic dissemination, standard publishing contracts, standardized manuscript preparation and formatting guidelines, and expedited production schedules.

More information about this series at http://www.springer.com/series/11467

Alain Ruttiens

Decision Making with Quantitative Financial Market Data

Applications, Precautions and Pitfalls

Springer

Alain Ruttiens
Department of Finance
ESCP Europe
Luxembourg, Luxembourg

ISSN 2195-0482 ISSN 2195-0504 (electronic)
SpringerBriefs in Operations Research
ISBN 978-3-030-67579-0 ISBN 978-3-030-67580-6 (eBook)
https://doi.org/10.1007/978-3-030-67580-6

This Springer imprint is published by the registered company Springer Nature Switzerland AG.
The registered company address is: Gewerbestrasse 11, 6330 Cham, Switzerland

To Adela Baho,
Andres Feal,
and Michel Godefroid,
with my gratitude.

Preface

Quantitative data are so attractive… just nice numbers ready for use at first sight. It is so tempting to handle them as they are in any kind of computations without seriously questioning their degree of precision, their pertinence toward the pursued goal, or about the way they have been extracted or elaborated. But they should be handled with care.

Although founded on rigorous bases, as well as on the professional background of the author, this booklet has not been written with the formalism of a scientific research paper, including traditional features such as a review of past literature, theorems, and proofs, etc. It must rather be taken as a tool for reflection, sometimes somewhat provocatively. Note that included numerical examples relate to the financial markets area.

In the following pages, besides a regular font, I am using:

- A smaller font for more technical, advanced developments
- "*Reminders*" boxes, with a smaller italics font for reminders of notions developed in usual textbooks (to be skipped by readers familiar with basic financial concepts, maths, and stats).

Luxembourg, Luxembourg Alain Ruttiens

Contents

Chapter 1
Basic Notions

1.1 Data: Quantitative Versus Qualitative

The Cambridge Dictionary defines a data (sing/pl) as an "information, especially facts or numbers, collected to be examined and considered and used to help decision-making, or information in an electronic form that can be stored and used by a computer."

A data is thus an information. The definition specifies it as "especially facts or numbers." We will therefore distinguish between *quantitative* data (numbers) and *qualitative* data (facts). Quantitative data, i.e., numbers, are suitable for some mathematical and/or statistical treatment, on the contrary to—at least, in most of the cases—qualitative data, figured by words.

This book concerns quantitative data, especially the way we should handle them in a safe, wise way. By contrast, qualitative data are not subject to the risks of misuses that form the content of this book. But they are subject to another type of risk, linked to a possible lack of clarification in the used words.

As a matter of fact, as said in the Foreword, quantitative data are so attractive because, first, the seeming accuracy of a number is more impressive than that of a word, or of a group of words. Second, referring again to the definition, because our activity is more and more assisted (dominated) by computers, which are obviously better adapted to the treatment of numbers.

However, for certain information, it is better/wiser to handle them as qualitative data than as quantitative ones (cf., e.g., Sects. 5.3 and 4.5). Interestingly, research in artificial intelligence is more and more working on qualitative data, despite the difficulties of interpretations.

As an example—one which involves both these types of data—let us consider the following case: somebody owes to pay you today a sum of $10,253.45, but he has not paid it. Qualitatively speaking, this is a payment default. Now, suppose he pays you the rounded number ($10,253.–): would you still consider this as a payment

A. Ruttiens, *Decision Making with Quantitative Financial Market Data*,
SpringerBriefs in Operations Research,
https://doi.org/10.1007/978-3-030-67580-6_1

default? Or, suppose he pays you the exact sum, but on the next day. Again, would you still consider this as a payment default? This issue can be solved if one specifies the "payment default" words by some more wording, typically a legal approach.

Actually, this simple example illustrates the dramatic case of the default payment risk in portfolio management, typically in a very usual portfolio of bonds. In the portfolio management business, securities markets regulators are obviously considering the default payment as a major risk. Unfortunately, since portfolio managers are used to handling numbers (quantitative data), and are willing to quantify the default payment risk, in a similar way as they (quantitatively) measure the market risk (the portfolio has gained, or lost, 5% in the last year), there is here a real issue: how to adequately transform a qualitative data into a quantitative one? To continue with the above example, paying later, or not the exact due amount, relates to the capacity of the debtor to pay, but a default payment can also result from a strategic decision (not to pay), hence the difficulty to precisely identify the default in terms of numbers. Incidentally, this problem is not yet solved in a satisfactory manner because of the difficulty to transform legal wording into numbers, but this goes outside the scope of this book.

Besides, there exists a particular quantitative treatment of imprecise, qualitative data, by use of *fuzzy numbers*.

> A fuzzy number is a set (interval) of numbers modeled by some function, which allows to substitute an imprecise number by a function, for uses in further calculations. Cf., for example, S. Chandrasekaran, *Applications of fuzzy number mathematics*, IJISET, vol. 2, issue 11, Nov. 2015.

Finally, the border between qualitative and quantitative data is very thin: consider for example credit ratings of the S&P agency, that is, a quality scale. Said credit ratings are applied to corporations and states, as debt issuers, and to their issued debt (bonds, loans). These qualitative credit ratings are split into 22 categories represented by letters[1], but they could be converted into numbers, for example from numbering 1 the best rating level ("AAA") to 22 the worst one ("D," for default).

By the way, the simplest qualitative scale is the well-known triplet ☹ 😐 ☺ . . .

1.2 Measure: Exact, or Not?

A quantitative data being a quantity, represented by some number, this number is resulting from some measurement: to measure consists of quantifying some size, in terms of some units of reference, and with some degree of accuracy.

If we consider a classroom, measuring the quantity of students present is straightforward. Let us suppose they are 20. Such counting is an exact measure. But what about the weight of one of them? At first sight, using a scale, the answer also looks

---

[1]Other credit agencies have a rather similar grid, with different symbols.

straightforward. Except that, given the scale used, the result can vary, depending on the degree of accuracy of the device. Each measuring device has its own limit in accuracy. As regards the weight of one of these students, we can for example obtain 78.6 kg. Taking into account the accuracy of the device, we could better tell, for example, 78.6 kg ± 100 g. The mention of "±100 g" determines the error margin of the measure, specific to the measuring device. In this example, the exact measure should be comprised somewhere between 78.5 and 78.7 kg.

Error margins play a major role in the conclusion we are tempted to draw from data. For example, if, in a political survey, it happens that Party A is expected to get 36% of votes and Party B 34%, concluding, at the date of the poll, that Party A would win over Party B depends on the error margin of the poll, that is, of the number of polled people (sample size).

Reminder 1.1: Explanation:
If the margin error of this poll (depending on its sample size) is, for example, + or −1.5%, we cannot say for sure that Party A is overtaking Party B. Indeed, the more complete information is

Party A: percentage comprised between 34.5 and 37.5%
Party B: percentage comprised between 32.5 and 35.5%

so that there is some possibility that the "real" percentages, which would appear for a much bigger sampling size, would for example be 34.5% for A and 35.5% for B: with these percentages, Party B is overtaking Party A.

Also, for many reasons, a quantitative data can be rounded. For example, if one wants to express $2,250,632.– in millions ("M"), we can opt for $2 M, or 2.2 M, or 2.25 M, etc., depending on the number of rounding decimals we keep. A big rounding is often preferred for clarity purposes (or effect of some advocacy), but we should not forget that excessive rounding can reduce the informational content of the data. But on the other hand, given the many reasons for handling data—in particular, measures resulting from models or formulas—which suffer from some error margin (as it will become clear from the next chapters), it may have no sense to produce outcomes of calculations with too many decimals. As a real-life example, I remember the "teaser" for a quantitative trading model, producing Sharpe ratios based on blank tests, with as many as five decimals!.

Moreover, if we combine in a calculation several numbers having been rounded with a different number of decimals, the accuracy of the final result is affected by the highest rounding.

We will later (cf. Chap. 3) revert on accuracy, in the case of measures that apply to a subset of data (sample).

In summary, handling quantitative data first implies to be aware of their accuracy degree.

Furthermore, to be appropriate, particular measures—such as risk measures, for example—must satisfy a set of properties, to be qualified as "coherent." This concept has been elaborated by Artzner et al., who consider properties of monotonicity, sub-additivity, homogeneity, and translation invariance. Despite this sounding obvious, it is not necessarily the case. For example, some usual measures, such as the Value-at-Risk (cf. Sect. 5.3), are however not coherent, because not sub-additive. Cf. Artzner, P.; Delbaen, F.; Eber, J. M.; Heath, D. (1999). "Coherent Measures of Risk". *Mathematical Finance*. 9, (3)

1.3 Differences, Spreads, and Percentages

Reminder 1.2:
Taking 2 data, 100 and 105,

- *the spread* $105 - 100 = 5$ *is called an* absolute *difference,*
- $\frac{105-100}{100} = 0.05$ *is called a* relative *difference, or, expressed as a percentage:* $= 5\%$.

In quantitative finance, the relative differences are also called *returns*.

There exists a rationale to prefer working with relative differences, or returns, to bypass the problem of data size. Consider the SP500 index varying as follows (end of years 2017, 2018, and 2019): absolute differences may, as here, significantly differ because the initial Index is significantly different over these 3 years, while (rounded) percentages, or relative differences, avoid this inconvenience because, whatever the higher or lower Index level, the scale of relative differences is almost the same.

	2017	2018	2019
Index:	2674	2485	3240
Yearly return (rounded):		−7.07%	+30.38%
Compounded return (rounded) on 2 years:			10.08%
Average of returns (id):			11.66%

As regards a global return on both years 2018 and 2019, one should distinguish between:

- The average of both yearly returns, i.e., the simple average of −7.07% and +30.38%: this cannot be viewed as the "average return," because both yearly returns refer to a different initial value, that is, −7.07% is from 2674, but +30.38% refers to 3240.
- And the global return on 2 years properly said, which is actually a *compounded* return (like compounded interest calculation).

Calculation of the compounded return, on a series of several yearly rates r_i:

$$\text{comp.return} = \sqrt[n]{[(1 + r_1)(1 + r_2)\ldots(1 + r_n)]} - 1$$

with here, $n = 2$ (years). Note that if one skips the nth square root, we obtain the whole return. Applied to this example:

$$\frac{\text{Index}_{2019} - \text{Index}_{2017}}{\text{Index}_{2017}} = \frac{3240 - 2674}{2674} = (1 - 7.07\%)(1 + 30.38\%) - 1 = 21.17\%$$

In assessing the comparison between returns or, more generally relative performances, one should go further than a simplistic comparison of the percentages. Consider for example the case of a portfolio of total NAV of 100, having two positions only: in asset A and in asset B, of 90 and 10, respectively. One month later, A has increased from 90 to 99, and B from 10 to 15. In terms of returns, A has increased by 10% only, by comparison with B having increased by 50%. But the contribution profit of A being +9 is however nearly twice as the one of B, so that restricting the analysis to the returns only is misleading.

Return measures: as an alternative to regular returns, "Quants" are rather using "log returns" (the reason will be given in Sect. 4.6), which are defined as follows:

$$\text{log return} = \log\left(\frac{P_{t+1}}{P_t}\right) \text{ with } P_{t+1} \text{ and } P_t \text{ respectively} = \text{price } P \text{ at time } t + 1, \text{and price at } t$$

Log returns somewhat differ from regular ones in the range of, say, 0 to + or to −20% returns: example from the above data: from 2674 (in 2017) to 2485 (in 2018), while the regular return is −7.07%, the log return is log(2485/2674) = −7.33%. But this is not a problem for analysis and research provided calculations do not mix both log returns with regular ones.

1.4 Data as Time Series

In many applications, collections of data are produced on a historical basis, hence the name of "*time*" *series*. Let us consider the case of prices or returns data. The successive prices or returns over time can follow a deterministic or a probabilistic one.

- Deterministic versus probabilistic time series

An example of a deterministic time series is the successive points in space, on the trajectory of a mortar shell. The gunner can easily compute the parabolic trajectory of the shell, to determine its impact with a high accuracy. Deterministic time series are predictable: in a deterministic world, the future is certain.

On the contrary, if we take daily prices of the SP500 Index, knowing the closing price of today does not allow forecasting the one of tomorrow, because the "trajectory" of successive daily closing prices is more or less random. Given the random nature of stocks (or any other assets) price evolution, a time series of stock prices is called a *probabilistic time series*. Probabilistic time series are unpredictable and the future is uncertain here. As the physicist Niels Bohr ironically said, "Prediction is hazardous, especially about the future."

In Sect. 4.2 we will discuss modeling such time series. One can build *predictive* forecasting models in a deterministic world, for example, the parabola of our mortar shell. But not in a random world. In this case, models do exist, but they can only be *explanatory* models, that is, ex post models.

However, the intuitive and convenient distinction between deterministic and probabilistic environments may be eliminated, at least in theory. The French mathematician Laplace has evidenced, as earlier as in the eighteenth century, that what we consider as "probabilistic" would yet be deterministic in the last resort: a probabilistic data should actually be a deterministic one, but with the impact of so many parameters to be quantified, that it is practically impossible to take all of them into consideration. For example, if we throw a stone from the top of a hill, we cannot forecast where it will stop at the bottom, but if we were taking into account all of the multiple factors affecting its trajectory, we should be able to.

- Continuous versus discrete time series

A time series can be made of continuous data over time. Back to our mortar shell example, its trajectory is obviously continuous. But time series can also be made of data that follow each other in a discontinuous, or discrete way. In our SP500 example, or even more on the forex market, during trading sessions prices are changing at a very high pace (even less than a second), looking continuous at first sight, but they are in fact discontinuous: they are just successive quotations, with a time interval which could not reach 0.

1.5 Usual Statistics on Data in Probabilistic Time Series

To finish with this introductory chapter, the behavior of probabilistic time series of data is quantified by statistical measures. Also, these time series will be analyzed with respect to the probability distribution of the data. Both statistical measures and related probability distributions will be widely used in the following chapters.

Hence, the following exceptionally lengthy "Reminders" # 1.3 and 1.4:

Reminder 1.3: Main usual statistics for time series:
To illustrate the following notions, let us consider a series of daily closing prices of the SP500, from August 21 to December 21, 2009, that is, 85 successive prices, with corresponding 84 successive returns. The two main statistics are:

(continued)

Reminder 1.3 (continued)

– *The* mean, *or* average*: the arithmetic average of the 84 daily returns is 0.00098.*

Like for interest rates, which are quoted in % per annum (whatever they apply on 3 days, 3 months, 3 years, or any other maturity), to facilitate the comparisons between rates of different maturities, returns are as well converted into % per annum (p.a.). The conversion is easy: considering there are about 250 business days a year, one just multiplies the obtained daily return by 250:

$0.00098 \times 250 = 0.24$,

that is, 24.5% p.a. If we use for example monthly returns, the multiplier would be ×12. That is, the result is multiplied by the number of periods in the year.

– *The* dispersion *measure, or* standard deviation*, which is here =0.01018, on a daily basis.*

Here too, one is used to annualize it, but for reasons explained hereafter, we must multiply by the square root of the number of periods:

$0.1018 \times \sqrt{250} = 0.319074 = 31.97\%$ *p.a. (rounded)*

In addition to these two statistics, we have to mention the variance*, which is the square of the standard deviation:*

In the example, the p.a. variance is $(31.97\%)^2 = 10.18\%$*. By the way, one can demonstrate that it is the variance that can be annualized by ×250, hence the way to annualize the standard deviation by* $\times\sqrt{250}$*.*

The variance is actually the average of the spreads between each data and their average.

– *Why the double measure of standard deviation and variance? Both are useful. The standard deviation presents the advantage to be added to or subtracted from a data (cf. several examples further in this book). The variance is more adapted to a rigorous parametrization of a probability distribution, but not much used in practice, though with some exceptions, such as in "variance swaps" contracts for example.*

– *In the language of financial markets, the standard deviation is called "volatility," and it is the most common valuation of a financial market risk.*

In the fund management business, the two key components of a portfolio performance—over some period of time—are its return *and its* risk*. One can observe that a return measure is a* directional *variable (a return can be positive or negative), while volatility (risk) is* not *directional: it is always a*

(continued)

Reminder 1.3 (continued)
positive number, whatever it refers to a risk of loss or a risk of gain. To illustrate this, let us graphically look at the performance (return and risk) of the Euro Stoxx 50 Index during the year 2016:

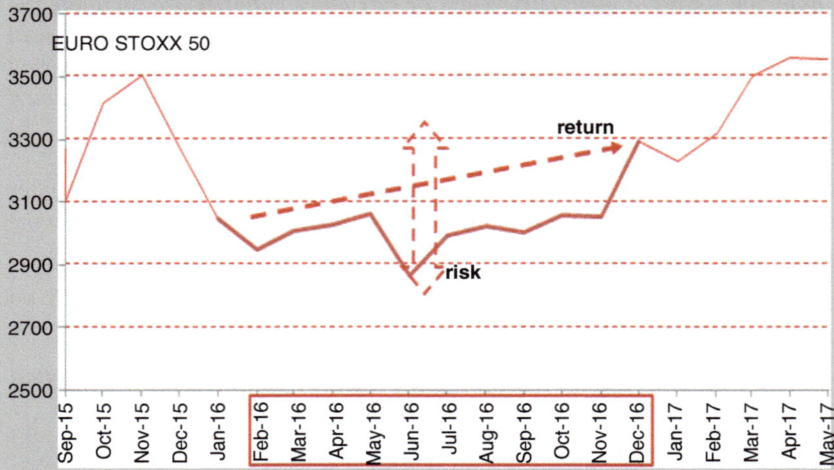

The return on that year was positive. But if the monthly data occurred in the reverse order (from right to left on the graph), that would result in a negative return, but with the same dispersion, or volatility:

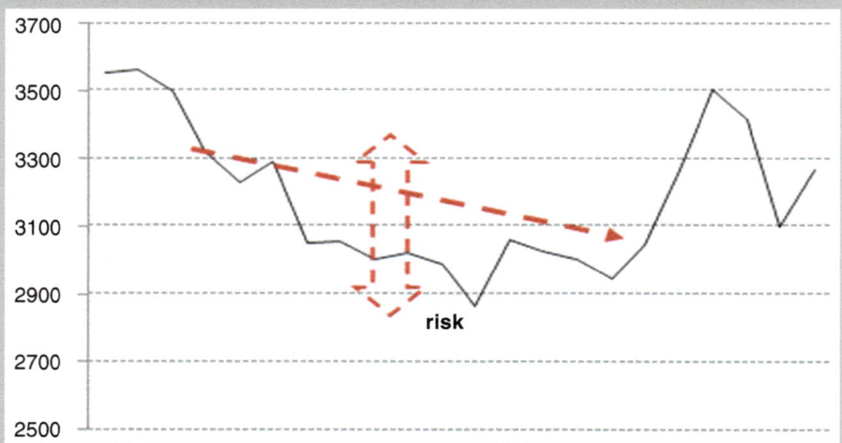

Reminder 1.4: Essentials about probability distributions:

– *The most usual probability distribution used for data in social sciences, and in particular for financial markets data, is the* Normal, *or* Gaussian *distribution, also called bell curve, given its shape:*

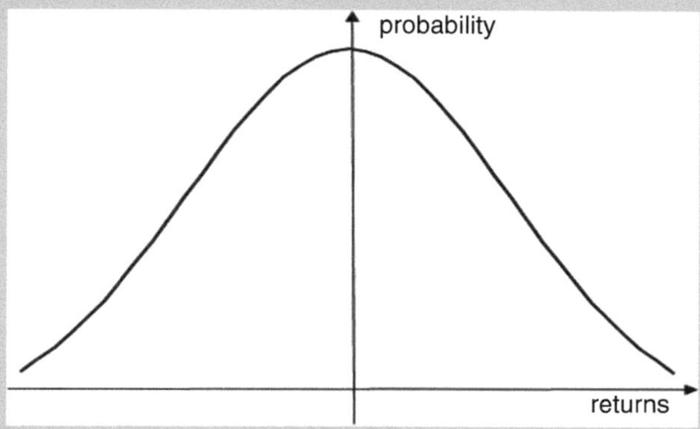

NB: In this figure and the following ones, the probability distribution is showed in function of returns values (on the horizontal axis).

The theory establishes that this probability distribution is fully determined by its mean and its standard deviation. This is convenient for us, since these parameters fit with our return and risk parameters. Positive and negative returns are located on the horizontal axis. The volatility is indirectly appearing from the shape of the bell (thinner or fatter around the vertical axis).

A major property of the Gaussian distribution is that about two-third of the range of returns is located within its mean +1 and −1 standard deviation:

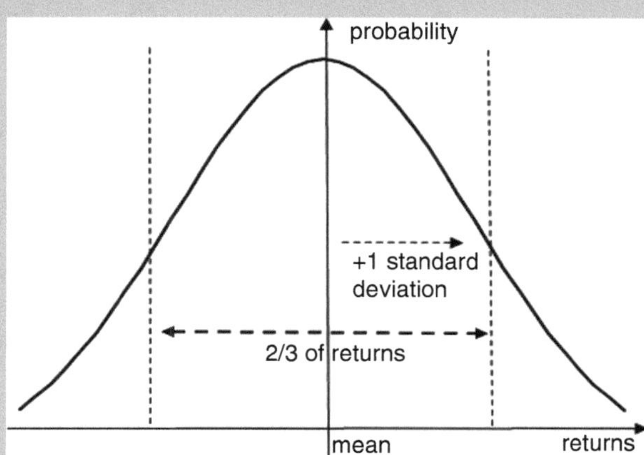

(continued)

Reminder 1.4 (continued)

Practically speaking, since data of financial time series are discrete (cf. the end of Sect. 1.4), representing the data like such a continuous curve is not possible. We have rather to group them into "buckets" (for example: from 0.1 to 0.2, from 0.2 to 0.3, etc.), leading to a diagram of frequencies (i.e., the number of returns per bucket) called "histogram." For example:

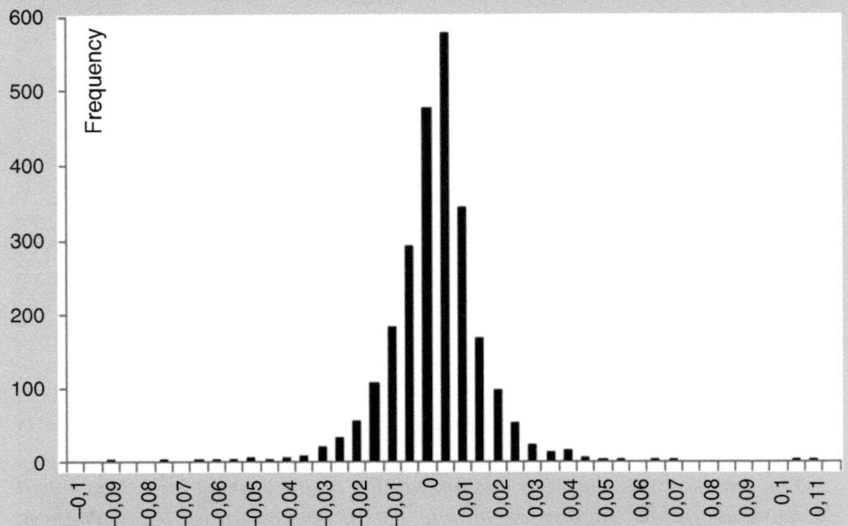

With a sufficient number of data, and by more and more shrinking the width of the buckets, the histogram moves toward the shape of the above continuous curve.

The advantage of the shape of the Gaussian distribution is that, to some extent, it fits with usual features of data in financial time series:

- *Higher positive and negative returns are less frequent than smaller ones.*
- *The curve is symmetric, that is the probability (50%) of positive returns equals the one (50%) of negative returns.*

Note, however, that if a Gaussian distribution is applied to returns, it implies the possibility of infinite losses and infinite profits (the distribution is not bounded, on both sides of the horizontal axis of returns), which is unrealistic, although to such infinite losses or profits correspond such tiny probabilities, actually moving toward 0 (on the vertical axis).

Moreover, in real life, time series of returns are almost never symmetric, thus not Gaussian (except, for some assets like stock indices, over a very long period, of dozens of years). But in many applications, we may want to reflect

(continued)

Reminder 1.4 (continued)
the fact that, ignoring if a market will tomorrow go up or down, it may be a cautious (wise?) way to translate it into a symmetric distribution.

More general distributions used with respect to times series of financial data are:

– Skewed distributions, *i.e., presenting some degree of asymmetry. Such a "skew" is said positive (negative) if the probability of positive returns is higher (smaller) than the one of negative returns. A good example is the "lognormal distribution," a positively skewed distribution, which is widely used to apply to stock prices data:*

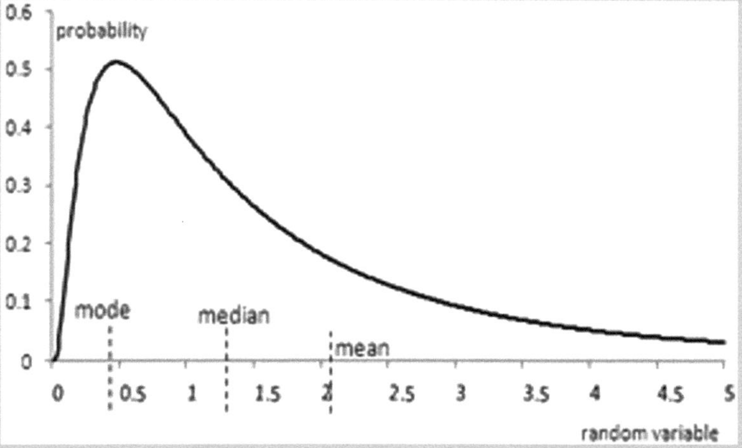

Contrary to the Gaussian, lognormal distributions are left bounded. In this figure, showing a positively skewed curve, the lowest value of the returns variable (noted "random variable" on the graph) is 0. Such a non-Gaussian distribution introduces two other measures, distinct from the mean, that is, the mode *and the* median. *For a Gaussian distribution, both merge with the mean value. The mode shows the peak of the distribution (not important within the framework of this book), and the median indicates the value of the variable such as the probability of having lower returns than the median is equal (50%) to the probability (50%) of having higher ones. The distance between the mean and the median thus shows the importance of the asymmetry. The median will be used several times further in this book.*

– *Distribution presenting some significant* kurtosis*: in some market circumstances, magnified during rallies or crashes, significantly very large positive or negative returns may occur with a probability much different than*

(continued)

Reminder 1.4 (continued)

the ones described by the Gaussian distribution. In this case, the distribution is said "leptokurtic," i.e., presenting "fatter tails":

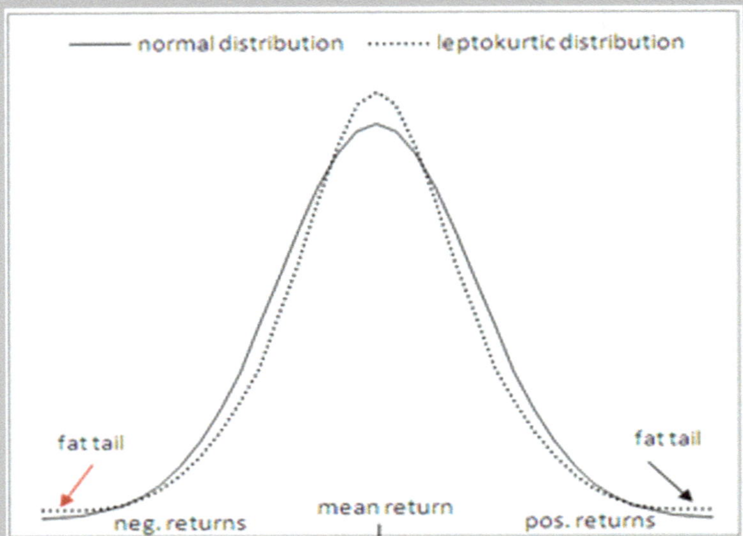

Here too, such a fat tails distribution will be used further in this book. Conversely, but less important for us, a non-Gaussian distribution can present flatter tails, then called "platykurtic."

Finally, one can also use more general distributions, presenting both some asymmetry and some kurtosis.

To be fully described, such a general distribution needs the determination of four parameters, called "moments," that is, their:

- *Mean ("M1")*
- *Variance (M2), → standard deviation*
- *Skewness (M3)*
- *Kurtosis (M4)*

instead of the two first only, as it is the case for the Gaussian one.

In short, the Gaussian distribution, because of its advantages and despite its lack of realism, may be preferred to more "sophisticated" ones, as it will appear further in this book. Indeed, for a time series of data, determining the parameters of a distribution is subject to some error margin, and four different errors can be worse than only two.

A key issue of the probability distribution is the determination of their tails, given the observed values of time series. In particular, in the case of prices and related returns, an observation, or data, which is very distant from the mean (such as a very big positive or negative return), called an "outlier," would of course affect these fat tails. But, do we have to consider such data as an error ("misquote") or not? And if yes, are we able to proceed with some "data cleaning"? Such concerns will appear in several of the following chapters.

Chapter 2
A Major Problem in Using Time Series of Data: Stationarity

As showed in Chap. 1, using time series of random returns implies representing them by some probability distribution, with at least their mean and standard deviation. The theory of probability establishes—beyond intuitive knowledge—that the more data we have, the more accurate will be the calculations, by reducing the error margin. In the case of financial market data, we can increase the number of data by going back in time. The need for a large enough set of data is even more crucial to adequately measure the possible kurtosis of a distribution, since extreme price movements and returns occur rarely, without taking account of some possible "outliers" (erroneous data or "misquotes"), and without having a satisfying method to distinguish an outlier from a true extreme data.

But financial markets activities, managed by people, fall within the social sciences. And human behavior, combined with the development of data collecting and data treatment technologies, does evolve with time. So that, going far back in time leads to aggregate heterogeneous behaviors. Moreover, even in a short time period, markets participants can vary in their way of acting (for example, going from a positive to a negative mood). As a consequence, increasing the length of time series of data is not necessarily a safe way for reducing error margins.

2.1 A Preliminary Issue: The Case of Data Frequency

In Chap. 1, we have shown that we can use data of different periodicities, such as daily, monthly, etc., and convert the result into "per annum" measures. At first sight, if on a series of data we compute their average return and their volatility, once converted into per annum measures (or % p.a.), the result should be the same if we have used monthly, weekly, daily, or higher frequency data. But this is ignoring that doing so, we work on a *sample* of the market data, which will affect the result!

A. Ruttiens, *Decision Making with Quantitative Financial Market Data*,
SpringerBriefs in Operations Research,
https://doi.org/10.1007/978-3-030-67580-6_2

Since market prices and corresponding returns are actually not continuous, the highest possible periodicity (using "tick by tick" databases, or as done in "high-frequency trading") is still a finite time interval. However, for going deeper in this direction, it is worth to have a look at the work of AÏT-SAHALIA, an attempt to answer the following question: to what extent the discontinuities observed in a series of discrete data are resulting from the discreteness of the sampling, or rather the evidence of genuine jump dynamics in an underlying continuous-time process? Cf. Y. AÏT-SAHALIA, *Telling from discrete data whether the underlying continuous-time model is a diffusion*, Journal of Finance, vol. LVII No 5, 2002, pp.2075–2112.

To illustrate this, let us take as an example, sets of the Euro STOXX 50 index data between June 23 and November 7, 2011, on a weekly (about 20 data), daily (about 100 data), hourly (about 900 data), and 5' basis, respectively (about 10,500 data)—5' being the shorter time interval stored by Bloomberg. Here are the returns and volatility, on a p.a. basis:

	5' data	Hourly data	Daily data	Weekly data
Sample size:	10,489	883	98	18
Average return, in % p.a.:	−19.57%	−23.27%	−47.33%	−29.30%
Volatility p.a.:	30.07%	29.04%	38.32%	38.88%

The results are different, both in returns and in volatilities. The impact of overnights and weekend is of course affecting the results. Note that overnights have not been included in the hourly and 5' data sets because prices changing from a close to the next open can of course more or less vary from one day to another, but in an order of magnitude which is not comparable with 5' or hourly changes (unless exceptionally, during strong market crashes or rallies). For sure, we could get other results by using another set of historical data than here (June–November 2011) (cf. next section). But one must recognize that almost everybody is using average returns and volatilities, converted into per annum percentages, without taking care of the impact of the periodicity of the used data! For the sake of completeness, we should not just compare the above numbers—what is although done by the vast majority of data users—but take into account their degree of accuracy. This will be developed in Sect. 3.3.

To go further in this matter, cf. W. Kinlaw, M. Kritzman, D. Turkington, *The divergence of high- and low-frequency estimation: Implications for performance measurement*, The Journal of Portfolio Management Spring 2015, Vol. 41, No 3.

2.2 The Problem of Stationarity

The probability theory defines stationarity in a very sophisticated way, but for the purpose of this book, we will simply say that a long series of random data is stationary if its probability distribution does not change along its time span, or more precisely, if its four moments (cf. Reminder 1.4) have the same value if computed on successive subperiods of time. Many random physical measures are stationary over time. Take weather conditions for example: even if the future air temperature is uncertain, at least its probability distribution, in a given place and at a given time is stationary, with a constant mean and standard deviation (at least up to a certain time, because of the climate change impact), so that one can forecast a future temperature (at +/− 1 week) to be observed around some expected known mean and with some expected known dispersion.

But time series of financial data are not stationary, because they are affected by human behavior. So that forecasting of financial data is not possible, even under some probability distribution, which is changing over time. Everybody concerned by investments is well aware that over time, mean, and volatility are varying.

To illustrate this non-stationarity, let us consider the SP500 daily data of non-annualized returns (in absolute numbers, not in percentage), from 1999 to 2009. The graph below shows how each of the four moments[1] are varying from year to year, also as non-annualized values. Needless to say, the presented results would be different on other ranges of years, and on other assets.

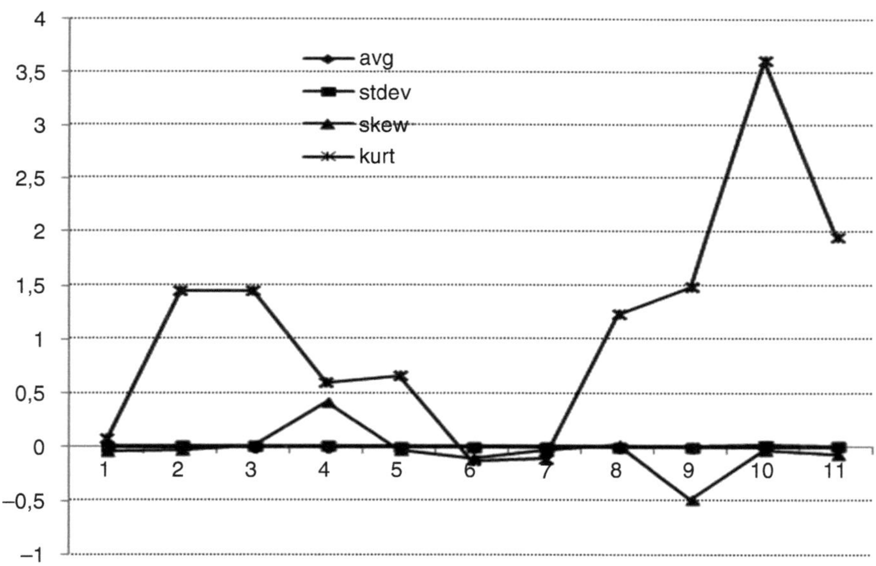

We can observe that higher moments M3 and M4 (skewness and kurtosis) are much more changing over time than the two first moments, which are almost not visible on the graph, due to the very wide common scale, for comparison purpose (on the y-axis, 1 is 100%).

By the way, we notice that:

[1]Actually, standard deviation instead of variance for M2.

- The skewness has been more often negative (the most one in 2007, not surprisingly—subprime crisis).
- The kurtosis has been positive, i.e., denoting fatter tails than in the case of a Gaussian distribution, except for 2 years (2004 and 2005) where the distribution was platykurtic rather.

Kurtosis values are computed "−3", i.e., by reference with the Gaussian distribution having a kurtosis = 3.

The dispersion over the whole period of 11 years for these 4 moments is indeed (remember that we have worked on non-annualized data and statistics):

Moments	Standard deviation of the 11 yearly results
Average:	0.09%
Standard deviation:	0.59%
Skewness:	20.49%
Kurtosis:	109.05%

At this stage, we can conclude that the higher the moment (from M1 to M4), the higher its volatility. This point will be revisited in Sect. 3.1.

As a conclusion, traders and portfolio managers being well aware of the difficulties to make forecasts, due to the variability of returns and volatility, it is unrealistic to hope for anticipating changes in skewness and in kurtosis. This explains why the variant of the famous CAPM of W. Sharpe, called as "4-moments CAPM" (although an understandable tentative for a more realistic approach that the Gaussian returns distribution used in the regular CAPM) is not applicable in the real life.

Chapter 3
Another Major Problem in Using Time Series of Data: The Accuracy of the Statistical Measures

3.1 Confidence Interval and Standard Error

Means (or averages), standard deviations (or volatilities), and other measures relative to probabilistic time series are to be viewed by taking into account some margin of error, relative to some degree of accuracy. Understandably, the greater the accuracy, the narrower the error margin, and conversely. This error margin can be quantified in two ways, which share something in common: the *confidence interval* and the *standard error*.

The Confidence Interval

Let us consider some probabilistic measure, related to a probabilistic time series of data. For such a measure, the confidence interval is a range of values that tells us, up to some percentage of probability, that the "exact," unknown value of the measure is located *somewhere* within this range. For example, the confidence interval at a level of 98% of a measured average of returns says that its exact value is located with 98% chances within the boundaries of some range. So that the narrower the confidence interval, the greater the accuracy of our measure and conversely.

This confidence interval, and corresponding accuracy, is mainly depending on the size of the data used for their calculation. Most data users are however not caring so far.

More formally, for a probability measure $\overline{p}$, the confidence interval of an observed value p of this probability, associated with an error α, is given by

A. Ruttiens, *Decision Making with Quantitative Financial Market Data*, SpringerBriefs in Operations Research,
https://doi.org/10.1007/978-3-030-67580-6_3

$$P\left(\overline{p} - \sqrt{\frac{pq}{n}} \times z_{\alpha/2} \leq p \leq \overline{p} + \sqrt{\frac{pq}{n}} \times z_{\alpha/2}\right) = 1 - \alpha \tag{3.1}$$

where $q = 1 - p$, n is the size of the sample used to compute p, and $z_{\alpha/2}$ is the z-score corresponding to $\alpha/2$. Note that this formula is applicable to a Gaussian distribution, but it suffices for our further developments.

Statisticians have elaborated more or less sophisticated tools ("statistical tests of significance") to assess the validity of a probabilistic measure, but this goes too far for the purpose of this booklet, which is not a textbook on statistics and probabilities.

More importantly here is the question of the size n of available data in our time series. Theoretically, if one computes a mean or other such statistics by using the whole set of all existing data, the obtained value is exact, but if it is not the case, i.e., if one uses a subset of the data, called a "sample" of size n, this will affect the accuracy of the result.

Let us start with an introductory example. Consider a set of so-called "random numbers," which are actually "randomly generated numbers," here generated by a Gaussian distribution of mean = 0 and standard deviation = 1 (called a "normalized Gaussian distribution").[1] If the size n of the set is not large enough, the average of the data sample will approximate but not equal to 0, same for the standard deviation ($\approx$ but not =1). Let us consider here four samples of n = 10,000, 1000, 100, and 10 "random numbers," respectively. We obtain,[2] in the case of a given generation of data (note that these results will vary each time we would generate another set of numbers):

$n=$	10,000	1000	100	10
Average:	−0.0027	0.0070	−0.0532	−0.1900
Standard deviation:	1.0037	1.0293	0.9598	0.9163

To these values of average and standard deviation will correspond some confidence interval, in function of the size n of the sample. Intuitively, the widest confidence interval will be associated with the smallest sample, the less representative of our probability distribution. Also, without going into the calculation of the formula, the intervals will also increase with the standard deviation itself.

Let us further calculate these confidence intervals on the obtained averages, at a confidence level of 99%.

The formula is

$$lb = m - N_{1-\alpha/2}\sigma/\sqrt{n} \qquad hb = m + N_{1-\alpha/2}\sigma/\sqrt{n}$$

[1]For sake of simplicity, we have used the Excel function NORMSINV(RAND()), which replicates a Gaussian distribution only approximately.

[2]For sake of readability, we have limited the obtained values to 4 decimals.

where *lb* and *hb* are, respectively, the lower and higher boundaries of the confidence interval, *m* and σ are the computed average and standard deviation, and *N* is the value (for $1\text{-}\alpha/2$) of the normalized Gaussian cumulated distribution. The spread between the two boundaries is clearly a decreasing function of *n* and an increasing function of σ. Note that for large enough samples, the use of the Gaussian is justified, given the asymptotic normality of the distribution of an average.

These confidence intervals will be such that, for each of these samples, the "true" average (or other parameters) will be located somewhere within its boundaries. These boundaries are centered on the results obtained above, plus and minus some quantity (determined by the formula). The spread between the lower and the higher boundary is thus defining the range inside which the true value of our parameter is located. And as said above, the intervals will be wider or thinner (with corresponding boundaries), depending on the value of *n*.

Note that in this introductory example, we know the true average (= 0) because we have deliberately built a time series based on a given probability distribution. But in real life, we ignore the probability distribution of our probabilistic time series. We will develop this in the next sections.

The results are:

$n=$	10,000	1000	100	10
Computed average:	−0.0027	0.0070	−0.0532	−0.1900
Lower boundary:	−0.0261	−0.0688	−0.2765	−0.8641
Higher boundary:	0.0207	0.0827	0.1701	0.4841
Hb – Lb spread:	0.0467	0.1514	0.4466	1.3492

Graphically, these confidence intervals look like.

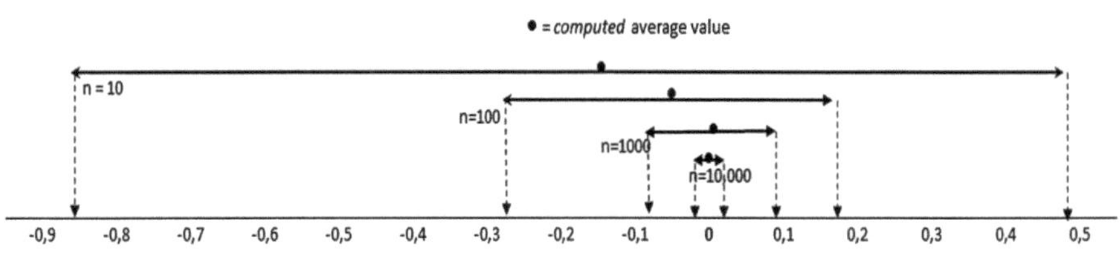

Hence, the importance of a large enough sample, if one wants a measure that is accurate enough. If we do not have enough data available, we must remember that our results may not be accurate enough, in view of what we intend to do with the measure.

Furthermore, the above calculation can also be used for determining the confidence interval of other parameters, such as the volatility, i.e., the standard deviation. The width of the spread will be the same as for the case of the average, of course now centered on the calculated standard deviation (this is resulting from the confidence interval formula).

Finally, the calculation of a confidence interval can also be used in reverse: instead of estimating the accuracy of a measure, given the size of the used sample of data, one can compute the size *n* of the sample which is needed to reach some accuracy level. This will be exemplified in Sect. 5.3.

The Standard Error

Another way of estimating the approximation of a calculated measure (average or others) is by determining its standard error. The confidence interval formula for calculation indeed involves the standard deviation and the size of the series of data.

In the above formula

$$lb = m - N_{1-\alpha/2}\sigma/\sqrt{n} \qquad hb = m + N_{1-\alpha/2}\sigma/\sqrt{n}$$

we see that both boundaries differ from − and + a term in $/\sqrt{n}$. Naming $\sigma/\sqrt{n}$ the "standard error," we have

$$\mathrm{lb} = m - N_{1-\alpha/2} \times \textit{standard error}\ hb = m + N_{1-\alpha/2} \times \textit{standard error}$$

So that the confidence interval and the standard error ranges differ from the $N_{1-\alpha/2}$ term.

We call "standard error" the value of 1 standard deviation, divided by the square root of the size *n* of the data series, so that we can determine an alternative measure of accuracy of a measure by the following range, say an average return:

average of returns – 1 std. dev. ↔ average of returns +1 std. dev.

standard error = 1 std. dev.

Formulas show that the range of −1 to +1 standard error is a much narrower range than the one of the confidence intervals for probabilities in the range of 90%. So that, on the contrary to the confidence interval, the range expressed with standard error cannot pretend to contain (or not) the exact value, at some probability level. Indeed, remember that the range defined by the confidence interval is depending on a percentage of probability.

Back to our introductory example, let us compare both ranges:

n=	10,000	1000	100	10
Computed average:	−0.0027	0.0070	−0.0532	−0.1900
Conf. Int., at 99%:				
Lower boundary:	−0.0261	−0.0688	−0.2765	−0.8641
Higher boundary:	0.0207	0.0827	0.1701	0.4841
Hb – Lb spread:	0.0467	0.1514	0.4466	1.3492
Standard error:	0.0100	0.0326	0.0960	0.2898
Lower boundary:	−0.0127	−0.0256	−0.1492	−0.4797
Higher boundary:	0.0073	0.0395	0.0428	0.0998
Hb – Lb spread:	0.0201	0.0651	0.1920	0.5795

We see that the spreads between the boundaries of the −1 to +1 standard error are about half of the ones of the confidence interval.

This is explained by the fact that for a confidence level of 99%, the normalized cumulative distribution is valuing about 2.3. Moreover, in the table, since we know by construction that we started from a sample of data generated by a normalized normal distribution, the standard errors indeed correspond to the standard deviations divided by the square root of the sample size.

We also notice that, for the four sets of data, having about the same calculated standard deviation of ≈ 1, their respective standard errors vary in a substantial way, that is, about $\times$ 30! (from $n = 10{,}000$ to $n = 10$).

In summary, the confidence interval has a richer informational content than the standard error, but the latter is more straightforward to compute, since in data treatments we always need the value of the standard deviation, so that it is widely used instead. Also, it is important to keep in mind that, if everybody masters the importance of a higher or lower volatility (standard deviation) in random data, the size of the data sample also matters, in a dramatic way.

3.2 Application 1

As a real market example, we can apply the confidence interval calculation to the non-stationarity of the two first moments (average and volatility), evidenced on a series of SP500 daily data, in Sect. 2.2. The database was made up of 11 years of about 250 daily data, from 1999 to 2009, and we obtained the following results, on the 11-yearly measures, but this time annualized, since the resulting standard deviations values are more "understandable" if expressed as per annum values:

Moments:	p.a. standard deviation of the 11-yearly results:
Average:	21.90%
Volatility:	9.29%

Regarding each of these years, the detail of the 11-yearly returns and standard deviations (whose values are not mentioned here) should be affected by some error, linked to the sample sizes of about 250 data. On the other hand, we can consider that the calculation of the "average of these 11 averages," that is, the result (21.90%) obtained for the whole set of 11 years, is error-free, since the series of 11-yearly data is not a subset of some broader series, but the full set (of 11-yearly data) itself. By "error-free" we just say that it is an exact measure of the average of 11 averages, but these 11 averages are not error-free.

So, here we have an *accurate calculation* based on 11 *nonaccurate elements* (the 11-yearly averages), which leads anyway to some inaccuracy.

Furthermore, the inaccuracy on each of the yearly returns will differ (despite the same sample size of 250 data), according to their own standard deviation. To cope with this, we will apply the principle that it is the highest inaccuracy among the 11 ones that will affect the global result (cf. Sect. 1.2). As it happens, this highest inaccuracy will be the one of the year which has presented the highest standard deviation[3] (recall that each year has been represented by a sample of the same $n = 250$ data).

We can thus use the largest value of yearly standard deviations in the calculation of the confidence interval on the global average of 19.61%, and on the global standard deviation. The result, for a confidence level of 95%, gives a range from 16.76 to 27.03% for the global average, and from 4.16 to 14.42% for the global standard deviation.

We can conclude that, at a confidence level of 95%, the "volatility" of the averages differs from the one of the yearly volatilities.

However, at first sight, one could be surprised that, contrary to the table showed in Sect. 1.2, now the standard deviation of the volatilities is lower than one of the averages. This is because we have worked here on annualized data ($\times$ 250 for the yearly returns, but $\times\sqrt{250}$ for the volatilities). But if one works on the yearly variances, its standard deviation becomes 146.91%, i.e., well higher than the one (21.90%) of the averages with a confidence interval. Moreover, the confidence interval (at 95% level) for the global variance goes from 141.78 to 152.04%, so that the earlier conclusion ("the higher the moment (from M1 to M4), the higher its volatility") still hold, in terms of no overlapping of their respective confidence intervals.

Finally, coming back to our earlier remark, saying that "Needless to say, the presented results would be different on other ranges of years, and on other assets" is indeed implying that results on 1999–2009 cannot, obviously, be applicable on other ranges of years, because they would involve other sets of data.

We have not pursued the analysis with confidence intervals on the global skewness and kurtosis, since their order of magnitude is so high vis-à-vis each other, and vis-à-vis the global average and standard deviation, that our earlier conclusion holds, that is, that the standard deviation of the yearly kurtosises is significantly higher than the one of the yearly skewnesses, which in turn, is higher than the one of both yearly average and standard deviation.

3.3 Application 2

Let us apply the same reasoning about confidence intervals to the example (Sect. 2.1) of sets of the Euro STOXX 50 index data between June 23 and November 7, 2011, on a weekly, daily, hourly, and 5′ basis, respectively. Here too, the question is: to what extent the measured values are inaccurate? And furthermore, given their

[3]Unsurprisingly, for those familiar with markets such as the SP500, this happened on the crisis year of 2008.

confidence interval, to what extent can we actually conclude that the average returns and volatilities do *actually* differ from each other? The results were:

	5′ data:	Hourly data:	Daily data:	Weekly data:
Sample size:	10,489	883	98	18
Average return, in % p.a.:	−19.57%	−23.27%	−47.33%	−29.30%
Volatility p.a.:	30.07%	29.04%	38.32%	38.88%

For this purpose, let us work again with a confidence level of 95%. By the way, the results hereafter are almost the same if we use other confidence levels, such as 90% or 99% for example.

This is due to the fact that the cumulative normal distribution is asymptotic to 1.

In summary, with respect to the average returns, the calculation of the confidence intervals leads to the following ranges:

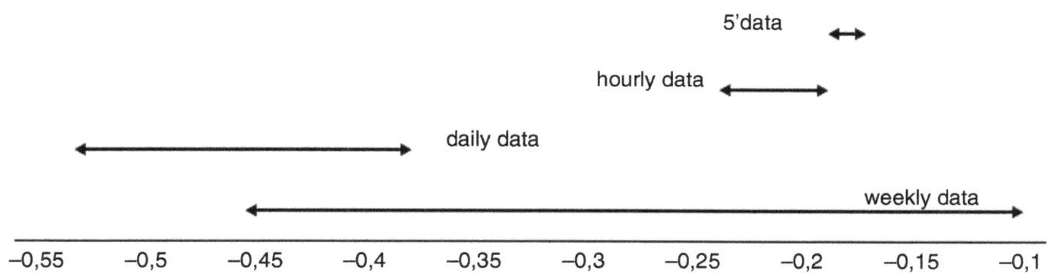

Unsurprisingly, the range is the narrowest when using more than 10,000 of 5′ data, and the widest when using 18 weekly data only. Two conclusions (at least about the present data, from 23/06/2011 to 07/11/2011!):

1. Skipping the weekly data (by far too wide range, due to too few data), we can deduct that, even if we ignore the "true" values of the average returns of the 5′, hourly, and daily data, these "true" value are anyway different from each other, in the absence of overlapping of the ranges (at least at 95% probability).
2. In practice, the use of samples of daily data is by far more usual. However, if applied to too short periods of time, as in this case (98 data) the resulting average value is far from accurate.

By the way, from the first conclusion and the graph, we also deduct that the higher the per annum periodicity, the lower the average return. Would it be always the case, on other sets of data? The answer to this question would need to test on other periods of time, but this goes out of the scope of this book.

Note that the same reasoning and conclusions about average returns also apply for the volatility (standard deviation) since, as already mentioned in the previous section, the widths of the ranges are the same as for the average.

As a more general conclusion, one should worry about the periodicity of selected data, to trust in average returns and volatility calculations. We will revert to this at the end of this chapter.

3.4 A Simplified Alternative to the Use of Confidence Interval or Standard Error

In many data analyses, one does not necessarily need a rather sophisticated calculation of confidence intervals. It is worth to apply what is called the "principle of proportionality." According to this principle, and applied here, depending on the complexity of an analysis and its objective, a precise calculation of error margin is not so important, hence the search for simpler alternatives.

In this respect, a practical alternative consists in adding to some measure the interval of +1 and −1 standard deviation computed on earlier data. Indeed, assuming data are distributed in a Gaussian manner, it is well known that cumulated probabilities between −1 and + 1 standard deviations cover about two-third of the probabilities. So that, at least if the Gaussian can be considered as a reasonable approximation, we can judge whether our measure lies within this range or not. Let us illustrate this with a simple example:

Consider XYZ Cy having achieved a first year of monthly sales (left scale) and corresponding cumulated sales (right scale), see graph below. For the second year, the Cy's target is at least to grow at the same pace (dotted line).

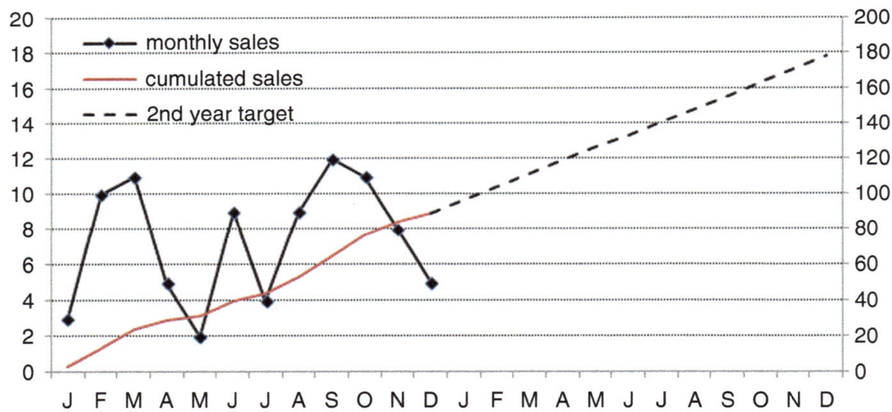

At the end of January next year, sales are so that, cumulated, they reach point B on the next graph. At first sight, one could claim that the January sales are above the objective:

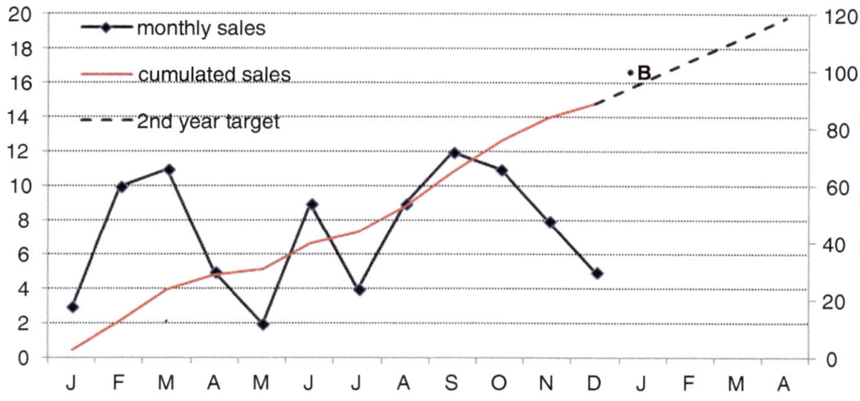

But the dispersion of the monthly sales during the first year (assuming it will be of the same level next year) is so that (assuming, again, that this dispersion is more or less Gaussian) B is below +1 standard deviation above the extrapolation, represented by the thin dotted line:

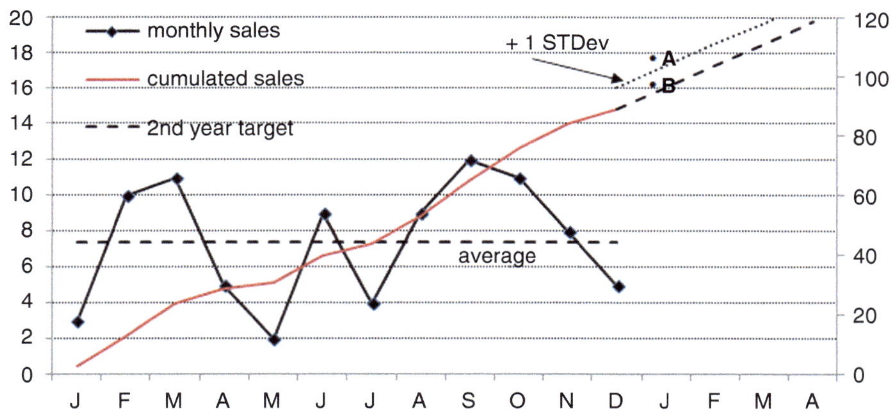

Instead of deducting that the January performance is "above the objective," we should rather conclude that it is just in line with it. If the January sales figures lead to point A instead, that is, above the "+1 standard deviation" line, in this case, the performance can indeed be considered as above the objective, roughly speaking. This reasoning can be renewed month after month, of course.

On the contrary, if the January performance is below the expectation line, such as point C below, it does not mean that it is a poor performance, since it is still above the "−1 standard deviation" line. One would rather speak of a poor performance if the January performance is at point D:

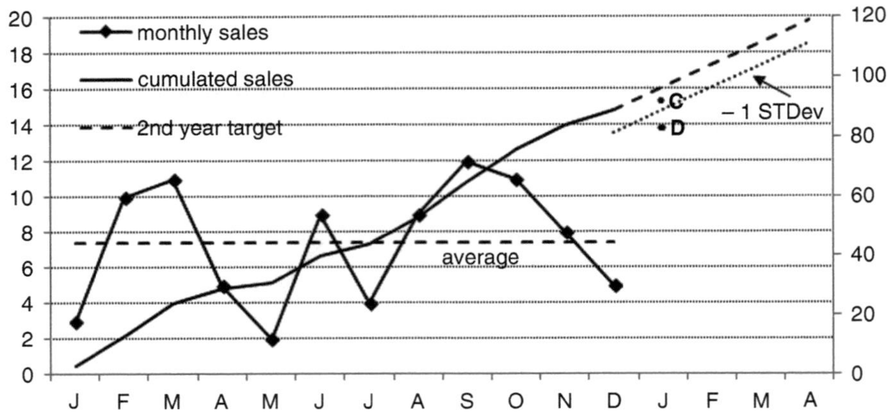

In conclusion, in any case of comparison between historic data and an objective, one should take into account the dispersion of the past data to assess a performance. This is valid, provided the distribution of past data is "enough Gaussian," and stationary enough.

In this spirit, it happens that graphical representations of financial price series are completed with two curves, located at +1 and − 1 standard deviation on both sides of the price curve. This raises the problem of both the stationarity and of the size of the sample used for computing the standard deviation. We will revert to this in Sect. 4.3.

Non-stationarity and Sample Size: Squaring the Circle?

In financial time series, the problem of the sample size is dramatically complicated in the case (almost systematic) of non-stationary time series, as considered in Chap. 2. Indeed, if, on the one hand, we need as much data as possible to reduce the standard error or confidence interval of our results, on the other hand, the more we will go back in time to enlarge the sample, the more we will be confronted to non-stationarity!

This is even more crucial with respect to modeling of market behavior or developing quantitative trading algorithms. This will be discussed—among other issues—in the next chapter.

Chapter 4
Issues About Modeling

4.1 General

Quantitative, financial models of any kind and for any purpose have in common the use of probabilistic time series, being therefore concerned by the points developed in Chaps. 1 and 2, that is, by stationarity and accuracy of the selected data. To these two issues, we ought to add a third one, that is to say, the quality of the model: to what extent is its output fitting with its objective, in an accurate way? This concern is called *model risk*. Indeed, any such model must be based in practice on a set of hypotheses as realistic as possible, destined to more or less simplify—to make it tractable—its formulation. All the more, for models in the field of social sciences, involving human behavior.

4.2 Modeling the Behavior of a Market and Related Valuation Models

As mentioned in Sect. 1.4, prices and returns being random, prices or returns models cannot be predictive, only explaining the market behavior in the past. Hence, asset prices and returns will need the use of ex-post probabilistic models. This is the case for spot products. Unconditional term products and conditional (contingent) term products (derivatives) are valued by using pricing models based, among others, on the modeling of their (spot) underlying price, so that these too need the use of ex-post probabilistic models. So that, in one way or another, as a user of derivatives you should have to be concerned about the validity of their valuation.

A. Ruttiens, *Decision Making with Quantitative Financial Market Data*,
SpringerBriefs in Operations Research,
https://doi.org/10.1007/978-3-030-67580-6_4

Reminder 4.1: Unconditional *versus* conditional derivatives
Derivatives, or term products, are contracts, concluded today, that set today the price of an "underlying" asset (stock, bond, currency, etc.), to be bought or sold at some future, maturity date. Such a future price is called a forward price, which differs from the current spot price.

Derivatives are unconditional if the transaction will unconditionally be realized at the contractually agreed forward price, regardless of the spot price traded at maturity. Main unconditional derivatives are forward contracts (traded on the OTC market), futures (traded on a derivative exchange), and swaps contracts.

Instead, derivatives are conditional if the transaction may or not *occur at maturity, this is the case of options contracts, for which the option buyer has the right, but not the obligation, to trade (at the earlier agreed price) at maturity.*

The valuation of derivatives is, among other factors, depending on the value of their underlying spot instrument.

- *fair price*

The first objective in modeling the price of any asset is to provide a *fair* or *theoretical* price. That is, what should theoretically be the value of it, regardless of prices actually traded in the market. If this is the case, it allows traders to refer to this fair price as a "reference," by comparison with the actual traded price, and, based upon this observation, decide to buy, to sell, or do nothing. The fair price can then be considered as objective or neutral. To reach this goal, the model producing such a fair, objective price must:

1. Be valid, grounded, and accurate enough—hence, the topic of this section.
2. Not be affected ("polluted") by market prices.

Therefore, regarding all of these models, I am making an important distinction between what I am calling:

- "Exogenous" pricing models, for which the modeled price is obtained by any kind of asset market prices, except by observed market prices of the instrument modeled itself
- "Endogenous" pricing models, for which, in one way or another, some observed market prices more or less intervene in the fair price valuation

This raises the problem of calibration. One should distinguish between:
- The case one builds a fair price model, then check to what extent computed prices are more or less in line with observed market prices (to detect some possible flaws in the model)
- The case the model includes some parameters which must be determined by applying it to (series) of observed market prices.

Needless to say, the second case is dealt with endogenous models.

Finally, the output of a pricing model will present some degree of inaccuracy, due to:

- The hypotheses used to build it (see below)
- The degree of (in)accuracy of the selected data

- *market price* vs *fair price*

Once a price has been modeled to obtain its fair value, it is interesting to compare it to its market value. As an example, remember the "dot.com" stock prices crisis in 2001. Some of these stocks had reached amazing prices, before a dramatic correction. During their bullish stage, prices went up through buyers who just considered that there was nothing to worry about. These buyers were of course the victims of the ensuing crisis. But others did not follow the excessive move, because they compared such excessive prices to stock pricing models (see below), reaching the conclusion that such skyrocketing prices were fully unrealistic (these would imply that, to explain them, the size of the market of the companies would have to exceed the whole planet).

In a nutshell, provided the market is liquid enough:

- The more the fair pricing model is grounded, the more (mid) market prices will turn around the corresponding fair prices. It may however happen that, in some circumstances (stressed markets) this link is broken.
- The bid–ask spread of the market price should ideally be wider than the degree of inaccuracy of the model. This remark is more specifically applicable to derivative prices.

- *modeling asset spot prices*

Textbooks are numerous about the valuation of market traded instruments such as stocks, bonds, currencies, commodities, etc. Like any kind of model, these are subject to more or less restrictive, simplifying hypotheses, and their validity as well as their accuracy is what it is, given these hypotheses. We will revert to some of them in the next section, dedicated to derivatives valuation, which involve underlying spot prices models.

Spot prices models are subject to accuracy problems, but not to stationarity problems provided they are used to value a current spot price, without conferring onto them any prediction capacity. As we will see in the next section, this is not the case with derivatives models.

4.3 Modeling Derivatives Prices

We can view derivatives models as a threefold construction: a model for the underlying behavior, the use of the yield curve (derivatives being term contracts, they all need to rest on a yield curve), the whole being covered by a model of the payoff of the derivative, given its contractual structure.

Reminder 4.2: The yield curve

A yield curve is a collection of interest rates of different maturities. Since all of these interest rates are expressed in the same way, that is, in % per annum, it is easy to put them on a graph, with respect to the set of corresponding maturities, ideally from 1 day ("overnight" rate) up to 30 years.

Example of a yield curve on German government bonds ("Bunds") and also on EUR swap rates ("IRS"), Nov 10, 2012:

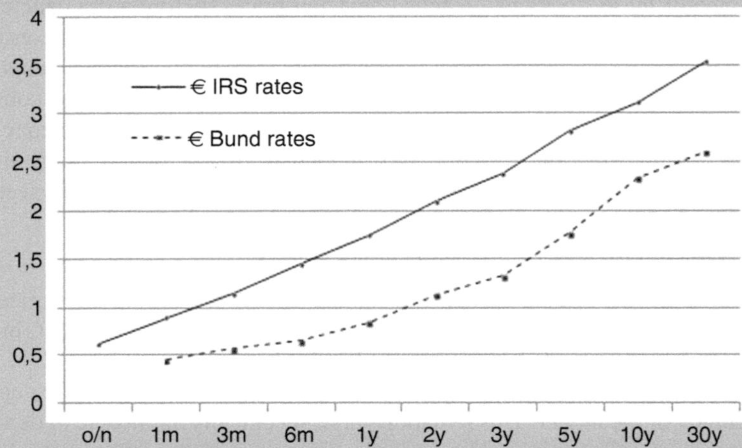

A correct yield curve must be homogenous in rating, such as government paper, or swaps interest rates, and homogenous in time. Since market interest rates are changing over time, it would be inappropriate to have a yield curve showing rates picked up at different times.

To go from the easiest to the most complex derivative models, we will distinguish between:

- Deterministic models of:
  - Forwards, futures, and swap contracts on usual assets
  - Interest rates and their yield curve
- And probabilistic (stochastic) models of:
  - Options
  - Credit derivatives

- *deterministic models*

By nature, deterministic models are not subject to stationarity problems. But rather, on the field of accuracy, i.e., the accuracy of the underlying spot prices.

As regards the model risk, deterministic models are by far the most reliable, since they are not affected by stationarity. All the more if they are exogenous models. One of the most familiar examples is the case of forward currency price, such as EUR/USD fair price determination. Its calculation needs the current spot price of the currency and two interest rates, in USD and in EUR, for the maturity of the forward contract, i.e., an exogenous model, with no model risk at all. However, for this forward contract as well as for other deterministic derivative models, these are still explanatory, not predictive models, since the underlying itself is random (the spot currency, in our example).

In this regard, it is worth insisting that a forward price cannot be viewed as a prediction of the future spot price at the date of the maturity of the contract. Indeed, remember in our previous example that the ingredients of this forward are pure current spot currency price and interest rates, which will change over time.

Furthermore, one should notice that such deterministic models are enforcing the no-arbitrage principle, which is the most radical way to reach a fair price that is not inconsistent with other market prices, indirectly involved in the forward valuation model.

Reminder 4.3: No-arbitrage principle

To build a suitable derivative pricing model, one assumes that the obtained fair price is equal to a similar result as the one which should be obtained by only using spot instruments. For example, the forward price of a bond will use the spot bond price, the financing cost (at market interest rate) of it, and the accrued revenue of the bond, the last two referring to the maturity date of the forward. Alternatively, one could buy spot the bond, finance it, and benefit of the accrued interest up to the forward maturity date. Applying the no-arbitrage principle imposes that both ways lead to the same result. Translated into (fictitious) data:

Let us consider a 3-months forward on a 10-year bond, currently priced @ 100 (% of par). The 3-months market rate is @ 4% and the coupon of the bond is @ 6% (= the current 10-year market rate):

- *Buying spot the bond, financing it for 3 months (let us round this at 0.25 year), and getting 3 months of accrued interest on coupon leads to*

  $100 + 100 \times 4\% \times 0.25 - 100 \times 6 \times 0.25 = 99.5\%$ *of par*

- $\rightarrow$ *The fair price of the future must be 99.5% of par*

so that the two ways leading to the same result, there is no possibility of "arbitraging" with profit between them.

As a result, it allows for traders to refer to the fair price as a "neutral reference," as explained in Sect. 4.2 above.

Finally, since deterministic models for unconditional derivatives are particularly simple and well-grounded, in normal market conditions the mid-market price will be in line with the computed fair price. But in case of huge market moves or expectations, significant differences may temporarily occur (as a recent example, market futures prices on the WTI oil, in April 2020).

Such differences are very easy to grasp for commodities futures, as they are translated into the "convenience yield" term. It is a pity that this convenience yield notion has not been extended to the financial futures—launched about a century later—calculations, where the difference between the fair price and the market price of the future is incorporated into the "implied repo rate" IRR. This situation is originating from the first years of development of financial futures markets, giving room for arbitrages ("cash-and-carry" or "reverse-cash-and-carry"), that have almost disappeared with liquidity increasing. The problem with the use of IRR is that a change of IRR involves both a change in the market interest rates (repo) and a change of market *vs* fair price, so that one cannot clearly extract the pure convenience yield effect.

- *probabilistic models*

With options, the problem becomes more complex because, as a contingent derivative, the payoff is depending on the underlying spot price at (or during) the maturity date of the contract. This needs to incorporate in the derivative pricing model, a probabilistic model for its underlying instrument.

There is a wide range of such probabilistic models, going from the most simple up to very sophisticated ones. Simple models are necessarily based on simpler, less realistic hypotheses than more complex ones. Experience shows that simple—but not simplistic!—models are more robust than others. A robust model is a model that is less subject to unsuitable outputs caused by the actual features of the market behavior. Robust models rest on the *principle of parsimony*, that is, they need to fix less variables, or less functions of variables—at least, the less difficult to determine—hence less error sources due to the modeling approach. Remember the French proverb: "le mieux est l'ennemi du bien."

In other words, a simple, robust model has more chances to perform satisfactorily in various market circumstances than a (too) sophisticated one, the same as, in a non-stationary environment a Gaussian (two moments) distribution will perform better than a four-moments distribution (cf. Sect. 2.2).

This observation seems not to be assimilated by everybody. For example, in the abstract of a Research Working Paper published by the Luxembourg School of Finance, one can read the following sentence (italics are own): "*Surprisingly*, we find that the GARCH structural credit risk model, *despite its more sophisticated approach*, typically *underperforms* more basic models."

The most widely used (because of its robustness) model for a time series of returns says that a random return (or price[1]) is made of the sum of two terms:

[1]The model for prices is a simple variant of it.

- A deterministic term, with a constant parameter being an "average trend," called "drift"
- Plus a probabilistic term, with a constant parameter of volatility of the returns, times a random outcome of a normalized Gaussian distribution

The model presented above is of course the general Wiener process, in returns or in prices,

$$dr(t) = \mu dt + \sigma dZ(t) \qquad \text{and} \qquad dS(t) = \mu S(t)dt + \sigma S(t)dZ$$

where notations are obvious enough. Note that, as an alternative to updating the constants μ and σ, we could rather prefer the more realistic Ito process

$$dr(t) = \mu[r(t), t]dt + \sigma[r(t), t]dZ(t)$$

except that it just extends the problem, since the $\mu[.]$ and $\sigma[.]$ functions cannot be modeled in a satisfying way, because of the non-stationarity. So that we are facing here the same problem as for the four-moments CAPM (cf. end of Chap. 3), making so that the Ito process is not actually applied by markets practitioners. Of course, as regards the $\sigma[.]$ function, there are volatility processes, such as the one of Heston, but introducing it into the Ito process, this adds a second stochastic term, hence the issue of the correlation between both of them. For more about stochastic processes, and also for mathematical developments in further "advanced" sub-sections, cf., for example, Alain RUTTIENS, *Mathematics of Financial Markets*, John Wiley & Sons, March 2013, 333 p.

Also, to cope with stressed markets conditions, the alteration of the constant σ into "smile" and "smirk" curves, while useful they are, they remain a pure empirical escape.

One step further, integrating processes like above, from the current time to maturity date of the derivative, needs the use of Ito's lemma; to the author's knowledge, this lemma is built within the framework of a Gaussian distribution of the returns. So what if one wants to integrate a non-Gaussian differential process?

A final note: Strictly speaking, one should distinguish a *model* from a *process*: a prices or returns *process* is the reality, which "quants" aim to *model* in the most satisfying way. However, in this chapter, we follow the common way of saying, such as "*modeling* s.th. by a Wiener (for example) *process.*"

This model raises two problems:

➢ First, a stationarity problem

Both the drift and the volatility (standard deviation) constants must be computed on past observed data, but:

- What about the size of the set of these past data? The more we go back in time, the more the non-stationarity.
- Since the model must be applied on the future date of the option maturity, later on, the actual trend and volatility will almost surely differ from the values used initially, again because of non-stationarity.

For example, in the case of daily Euro Stoxx 50 index prices, a way to illustrate the impact of this aspect of non-stationarity is by confronting, as in the graph below, the series of index prices (covering years 2011 and 2012) with the range (right side scale) of the drift at +1 and −1 standard deviation (volatility), both p.a. drift and volatility having been computed on the 50 previous days:

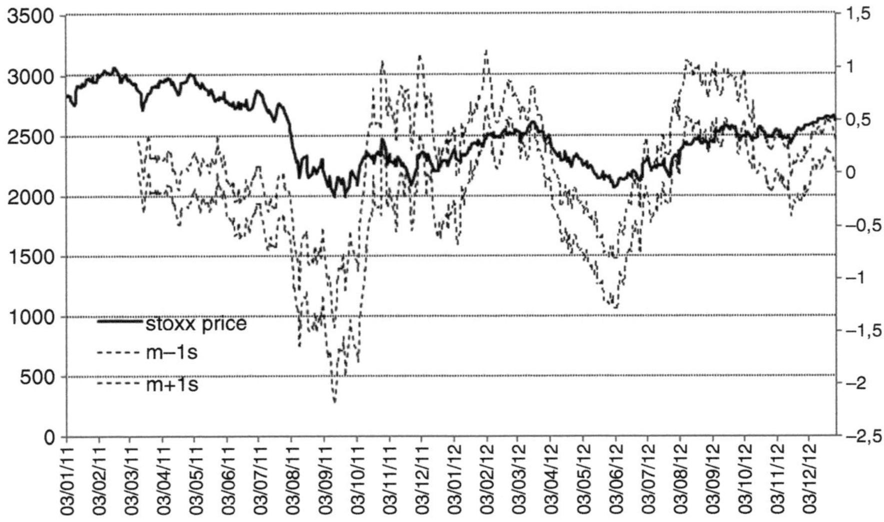

Considering as a first approximation that the range is a kind of error margin around the drift (returns average), we observe that:

- As regards the level of the range, and thus of the returns average, it is significantly varying over time, from negative to positive values (not surprising, since all financial markets show successive periods of upward and downward moves). Hence, the difficulty to select an adequate size of the set of returns for the average calculations, since using other sizes than 50 data would show a different pattern.
- As regards the width of the range—a 2 standard deviations spread—it is also significantly varying over time, so that the above difficulty also applies for the volatility.

Both these observations are nothing else than translating the non-stationarity of the time series, in terms of average and standard deviation.

Therefore, practically speaking, to quote an option, the market maker will have to select which drift and which volatility he will use for pricing. His choice will of course be based to some extent on the values issued from the past time series, but adapted at best, depending on his market experience. So that, in practice, these two "constants" are paradoxically not constant, they will rather be updated at each time of a new quotation.

➢ Second, an accuracy problem, resulting from the size of the past time series used for computing a reference basis of drift and volatility, which will be determined with some error margin, as shown in Chap. 3. Practically speaking, to cope with this, the quoted mid-price of the market maker, being spread between a *bid* and an *ask* price, it would be good that the spread be wider than the error margin on the mid calculation.

In practice, even if this constraint is not that much checked, usual options markets run satisfactorily, and one frequently observes widening bid–ask spreads during market stress periods. But this is not necessarily the case, for example with complex "non-vanilla" options, or on newly launched markets, with no liquidity yet and no history of past transactions. In this last case, it can explain why in some circumstances a market maker will not even quote a two-way price.

But globally speaking, one must recognize that the market practice is not going up to ensuring bid–ask spreads are actually coherent with error margins originated by lack of accuracy resulting from the too small size of time series of underlying prices and returns. In particular, we should worry about narrowed spreads caused by competition among market-making firms.

To go further with derivative pricing formulae, it is worth to notice that starting with the above process and applying the no-arbitrage principle (cf. earlier in this section) leads to an option price using the (riskless) market rate instead of the calculated drift on the underlying model. At least, this contributes to reduce the non-stationarity risk. This is valid for pricing an asset delivering no revenue during the lifetime of the option (for example, on a stock, if no dividend is paid during that period; or on a commodity).

But as soon as the valuation formula is involving a revenue paid during the lifetime of the option, the obtained price is subject to the validity of any anticipated revenue. For an option of a stock, if its maturity involves a known, future dividend payment, no problem. If the maturity of the option occurs on the next year, one can still consider that the next year dividend(s) can be reasonably estimated. But this raises the question about options on longer maturities, for which the anticipation of future revenues is much more questionable.

To go a step forward, without entering in their mathematical formulation, the robust model introduced above, as well as others developed on a similar basis, but more complex (and less robust) are expressed as "differential equations," which means that they are starting as a formula valid for a tiny time interval, actually tending to 0 (called "instantaneous" time interval), and in a next step, integrated to a finite time interval, such as up to the maturity date of an option.

Again, without entering in mathematical details, the integration step needs to be applied on a continuous function, that is, existing continuously, at every instant of time. Yet, since market prices and corresponding returns are actually not traded continuously, the smallest possible time interval (consider for example the "high frequency trading"), which can be much shorter than a second, is still a finite time interval. Fortunately, this obstacle has been mathematically overcome, allowing for tractability of the pricing models.

Overcome: by use of the Ito lemma.

It is further worth noting that, beyond the issues of accuracy and non-stationarity, the "robust" models considered here are subject to the validity of their underlying hypotheses (cf. textbooks for more details). Among these, the hypothesis regarding the *liquidity* of the market gains more and more in importance, at least in terms of risk management.

Finally, as regards derivative pricing built on *endogenous* models, they cannot be accepted as fair prices, because they are to some extent depending on some related market prices observations. At least, such models are to be considered as presenting a model risk, in the sense of a risk management approach (cf. Chap. 5). To keep a rigorous approach, one should consider exogenous models not as leading to a fair price, but to be used as a decision help tool, not more. This will be exemplified in a further section, about credit derivatives.

4.4 Using the ARCH Family of Processes in Derivatives Modeling

The rich ARCH family of processes is built upon two simple blocks:

- An AR(p) (for "AutoRegressive") process, expressing in a nutshell a return as a sum of p previous observed returns, plus a random error term. To some aspects, this more or less recalls the robust probabilistic model we have presented in the previous section.
- An MA(q) (for "Moving Average") process, considering that a series of pure random returns can be modeled from a series of randomly selected numbers. It supposes that the last randomly selected number is a function of errors resulting from q previous differences between last numbers and the preceding ones. In other words, so that, to the extent that a return is random, it could be explained by such a process. Note that the simple concept of moving average is widely used in other forms, cf. Sect. 4.8.

Without going further on this direction, it is enough to understand that both AR and MA will be affected by non-stationarity, as well as by some inaccuracy resulting from the selected length (p or q) of the series of past data. Moreover, as regards the AR(p) process, one can demonstrate that its "memory" in infinite, which is hard to accept as regards the problem of non-stationarity. By contrast, the AR(q) process has a memory of q.

From these two building blocks, researchers have developed a lot of more and more sophisticated processes, also involving the random nature of volatility over time, under the name of famous ARCH and GARCH processes. But all of them are subject to the same weaknesses of the two initial building blocks, namely as regards non-stationarity and (in)accuracy, and all are confronted to the problem of adequately determining the length of the series of past data.

I personally consider this family of processes very enlightening for a deeper understanding of the probabilistic nature of financial time series, but not robust enough to be accepted in derivative pricing. At the risk of sounding provocative, said in other words, the ample scientific literature about this family of processes just shows that some academics have found here an unlimited research field to help them publishing papers. It suffices to say that today the ARCH/GACH family counts more than 150 variants of models. To revert to a "politically correct" language, the ARCH family would rather be used as a decision help tool than as a derivative pricing model.

4.5 Modeling Credit Derivatives Prices

This section is on credit derivatives ("CDs" further in this section) named CDS (credit default swap), TRS (total default swaps), and several others, also denominated "swaps." Swap pricing belongs to the class of deterministic models (cf. Sect. 4.3). But, even though credit derivative instruments are labeled "swaps," they are actually "conditional swaps" (i.e., one or both legs of the paid cash flows is conditioned to some event, namely the occurrence of a default payment), which are actually options products. They have therefore to be valued with a probabilistic model.

The underlying of all kinds of CDs is the risk of default, of a debt, or of a company or a State. Very unfortunately, elaborating an option-like CDs valuation model is facing several major issues:

- First of all—fortunately for investors—a default is a rare event. Yet, probability distributions and related statistics are uncomfortable with rare events. Indeed, the default risk is located in the left tail of a probability distribution, which is uneasy to deal with. NB: this point will be somewhat developed in Sect. 5.2, in a section dedicated to VaR.
- The underlying of an ordinary option is any kind of financial instrument, related to any kind of asset, which can be determined by its *price*, that is, by a *quantitative data*. On the contrary, the underlying of a CD, namely the default situation, is the *occurrence of an event*, that is, a *qualitative data* (remember Sect. 1.1). It is obviously hard to convert a qualitative into a quantitative data, needed for being used in a derivative valuation. Moreover, the notion of event of default, as a qualitative data, is covering a lot of subtle shades, with a sophisticated juridical flavor, carefully drafted by the ISDA organization. To the extent that, in order to strictly (for example, contractually) talk about a "risk-free" or "non-defaultable" bond (such as a bond issued by an OECD country), one preferably uses the expression "a bond, non-defaultable under the sense of ISDA."
- Ordinary options are not so easy to model for pricing, yet they refer to a single variable, that is, the underlying price of an asset (or a basket of assets). But to quantify the underlying of a CD on a given debt needs a *double* information:
  - What is the probability that this debt will default?
  - In case of default, what is the value of the debt after default? (this depending on the value of the assets in the balance sheet of the company),

  so that it needs to be quantified by two numbers instead of one.

- Pricing models need to rest on a set of hypotheses, which simplify the problem in order to make it mathematically tractable. The issue is that the more the underlying price behavior is complex—as it is the case with default—the more the hypotheses risk to be too reductive and/or restrictive, to still be realistic.
- A CD contract must refer to a specific debt (called "reference obligation"), so that the market is expected to trade much more CDs underlyings than options do. As an example, take a major company like General Motors: there is one GM stock, hence, one stock option underlying, but the company has more than 100 subsidiaries, each of them having several bank loans, some of them having issues of bonds, subject to be selected as different reference obligations, therefore, many possible CDs underlyings.
- For the above reason, the vast majority of CDs are traded with a very low market liquidity, although among above pricing model hypotheses, the hypothesis of market liquidity is always a must. NB: a major exception are CDs on market indexes, such as CGX and iTraxx, which are very liquid.
- Finally, by using market data with respect to a credit default risk, the impact of a possible default risk, such as a risk premium on a bond yield, is actually mixed with the liquidity risk of the bond, which for its part affects the risk premium as well. And there is of course no way to share such a risk premium between these two causes.

So that, unsurprisingly, we can fear that the output of CDs valuation models would not be satisfactory, in terms of accuracy. This category of models is probably presenting the best example of model risk. Indeed, there are several types of "theoretical" CDs models, involving for example time series of issuer stock price (ex: KMV model), or typical binomial approach as used in ordinary option pricing, or involving a GARCH process, etc.

Hence, given the weaknesses of these models, market practitioners are rather using "practical" models (such as CreditMetrics and CreditRisk+, among others) resulting from data mining and data crunching techniques, applied to many observed market data of all kinds. These techniques, for sophisticated they are, cannot be considered as "models," in the sense of the models mentioned in the previous sections. Furthermore, their output cannot be taken as a fair price. They must rather be viewed as "pricing tools," based on a set of statistical treatments of data, which could probability be even improved in the future by the use of "big data" techniques.

We could also criticize the fact that the above "theoretical" models are using the output of "practical" pricing tools for calibration purpose.

Given the difficulties inherent to CDs valuation, it would be unfair to criticize the weaknesses of existing pricing tools. However, too often, traders consider outputs of such pricing tools just in the same way as fair prices outputs of true pricing models, and trust them accordingly, instead of using them as decision help tool in their trading decision.

4.6 Use of Non-Gaussian Distributions in Modeling

We have already emphasized the risk of building a more complex model, in particular by incorporating skewness and kurtosis, with the laudable intent of better taking account of a more realistic, non-Gaussian, world. We mean, leading to a too sensitive (among others, to non-stationarity), less robust model, passing over the parsimony principle.

But, in some cases, a non-Gaussian probability distribution is unavoidable. For example, the distribution of asset prices (not returns!) is all but Gaussian. Fortunately, if we go back to the returns model presented above, with its partially deterministic and partially Gaussian components, it leads to a non-Gaussian distribution of corresponding prices, called "lognormal."

Integrating the general Wiener process expressed in returns

$$dS(t) = \mu S(t)dt + \sigma S(t)dZ$$

where Z is a normalized Gaussian distribution, leads to a lognormal distribution of "log returns," which, in turn, leads to a lognormal distribution in prices:

$$S(t) = S(0)e^{\left(\mu - \frac{\sigma^2}{2}\right)t + \sigma\sqrt{t}Z(t)}$$

which at least looks realistic, downwards bounded to 0 and not bounded upwards:

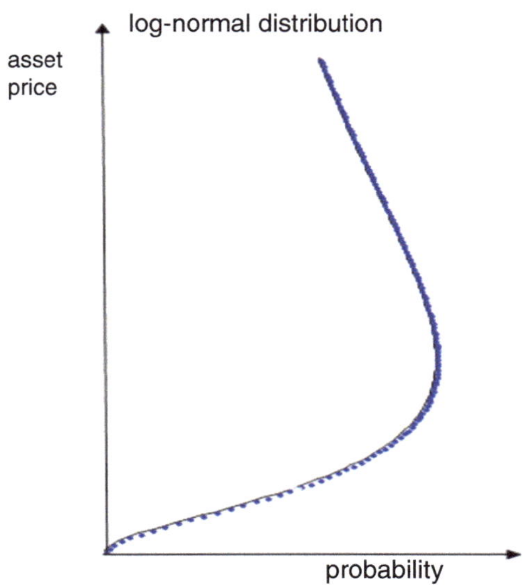

More generally, if we have to use a series of outputs of a non-Gaussian probability distribution, or to deal with a series of data that are at least somewhat significantly skewed, which implies that they are distributed in a non-Gaussian way, we should be careful not to take the mean of such distributions, but rather the median! (if needed, go to previous *Reminder 4.1*).

This is to minimize the error made on the measure taken from a skewed distribution. Indeed, by definition, the median of a distribution is such that there is a 50% probability that the "true" unknown value is above the value of the median, and 50% probability that the "true" unknown value is below, so that by selecting the median, we minimize the error ≡ |"true" value − median| : there are same chances that the "true" value is above or below the median. This would not be the case if using the average, because, due to the degree of skewness of the distribution, the probabilities on both sides of the average are uneven, so that there are more than 50% chances, with the average, to be located on the "wrong side" (too high or too low) vis-à-vis the "true," unknown value.

Incidentally, this way of working seems not always to be followed. As an example, among the various ways to price an option, typically in the case of a "non-vanilla" complex option, the "last resort" methodology, called "Monte Carlo simulations," consists in randomly simulating several thousands of time the payoff of this option. Strangely enough, the common procedure of Monte Carlo ends by taking the average of the outputs of these many simulations. Yet, the thousands of simulated option prices are distributed in a non-Gaussian way, so that one should rather use the median of the results. By using the average instead, the greater the skewness of the distribution of the simulated option prices, the greater the size of the error.

It is worth to notice that the median plays an important hidden role in a forward calculation. In a Gaussian returns environment, leading to a lognormal distribution of forward prices, the median of the lognormal is indeed the best guess, as minimizing the error vis-à-vis any other value. The parameters of both these distributions are

	Normal distribution (returns):	Log-normal distribution (prices):
Mean:	m	$e^{m+\frac{\sigma^2}{2}}$
Median:	m	e^{m}
Variance:	σ^2	σ^2

So that the best guess for a forward price of maturity T of a spot (at current time t) price S_T is the median:

$$F_t = S_t e^{mT}$$

In a "risk neutral" (with superscript "Q") world, with $m =$ the market rate r for maturity T, it becomes

$$F_T^Q = S_t e^{rT}$$

which actually has the form of a traditional forward price calculation. Hence, the rationale for using a forward price: among all other possible, unknown S_T prices, the forward is the one minimizing the error with respect to the future reality:

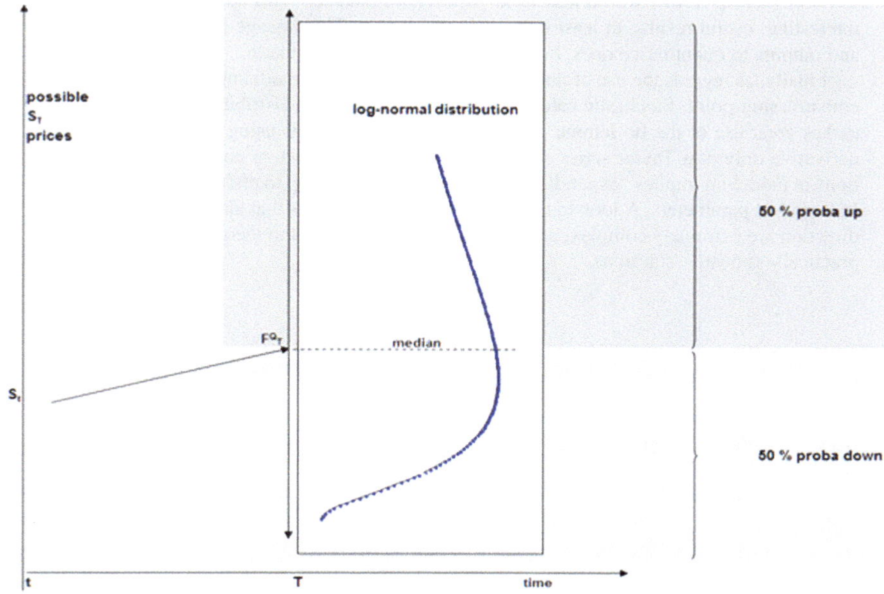

This justifies that in all the situations in which we have to cope with future values of prices, we meanwhile use their forward valuation. The same for interest rate swaps calculations, where future, unknown LIBOR[2] rates are replaced by forward interest rates values.

4.7 Use of Non-Gaussian Distributions in Modeling: A Step Further

Researchers have developed many tools to cope with non-Gaussian distributions, such as jump processes, Gamma processes, mixed processes (Wiener + Poisson), all of them being specific cases of more general Levy processes. Besides, they have also developed fractional Brownian motion, regime-switching models, etc. Practically speaking, applying such models needs using Monte Carlo simulations. For further reading, cf. for example E. JONDEAU, S.H. POON, M. ROCKINGER, *Financial Modeling under Non-Gaussian Distributions*, Springer, 2010, 560 p.

We should also mention attempts of using neural networks, as non-parametric forecasting tools. However, one cannot say that in the case of financial markets data this approach has been convincing, up to now. The main obstacle is, once more, the non-stationarity of time series of data as input of neural networks. So that, for handling non-stationary times series of data, to operate properly with neural nets would necessitate—as a first "layer" in the process—to build some "sorting device," sending separately each specific regime to its dedicated neural net tool. Once more, it is easier said than done.

[2]Waiting for its SOFR successor, as regards the USD interest rates.

Going a step further would lead us to "behavioral finance." This approach has produced interesting, useful results, at least in a *qualitative* sense. The passage from qualitative data and outputs to quantitative ones, however, seems really problematic.

Finally, as regards the use of non-Gaussian distributions in modeling, we should raise an embarrassing point. Stochastic calculus is built on a Gaussian distribution assumption and makes great use of the Ito lemma. Coherently, the Ito lemma is using on up to the second derivative only of a Taylor series expansion. So that the passage to non-Gaussian distributions in modeling implies "expanding" the stochastic calculus up to distributions needing the M3 and M4 parameters. A look to the academic literature shows that alternative ways in this direction are extremely complex, and probably too formal and too theoretical for producing practical—robust!—solutions.

4.8 Other Potential Troubles with Derivatives Valuation

- *options delta hedging*

For readers concerned by the management of a book of options, actually, as a market maker, there is a very first, well-known practical issue, namely the impossibility to apply a continuous, dynamic option replication, as it should theoretically be performed in "delta neutral" hedging, since option pricing models have been based on continuous differential equations. So that, even if a fair price is correctly determined, it would however not incorporate the consequences of its implementation, in a discrete (not continuous) world.

Theoretically, if an option position is continuously hedged by the market maker, at maturity the (mid) monies paid or received through continuous delta hedging should equal the mid option premium (another example of no-arbitrage condition). Since it is impossible to replicate this condition in discrete time, one could imagine to propose an option contract which, instead of being paid (by the option buyer) the option premium upfront, computed from the option pricing model, the premium would be paid at maturity, but on the basis of the actual cost of successive, discontinuous delta hedgings, according to a contractual scheme. The result would be fairer for both parties, but practically hard to implement.

To summarize, we thus face here the case of a model producing a satisfying fair price, whose consequences are not so fair.

- *autocorrelation*

But a more general, potential trouble, not sufficiently taken into account by market practitioners, is related to *correlation* problems.

Reminder 4.4: Correlation and autocorrelation

The (coefficient of) correlation between two time series of data measures to what degree they evolve in the same way. This coefficient can vary from +1—perfect correlation—if both series behave exactly in the same way, to −1—inverse correlation—if each one behaves perfectly in the reverse way as the

(continued)

Reminder 4.4 (continued)
other one, passing through 0—no correlation at all, or pure decorrelation—if each of them behaves fully independently of the other one.

In the case of more than two time series, the coefficient of correlation is necessarily measured 2 by 2 ("pair correlation"). As an example, a stocks portfolio manager can quantify the degree of correlation among each of the stocks of the portfolio by measuring the correlation of them, 2 stocks by 2 stocks (the result, being a set of correlation measures, is called a correlation matrix). This task is crucial for the portfolio managers to the extent that, as everybody knows, the more a portfolio is diversified (that is, presenting low pair correlations), the less volatile, hence less risky it is. This has been precisely formulated in the "portfolio theory," leading to the Markowitz and Sharpe CAPM.

Correlation explains why the volatility (standard deviation) of a stock index is lower than the combination of volatilities of individual stocks belonging to the index.

Without entering into the mathematical treatment, we can link the correlation concept to a "covariance" concept, that is, not the variance of a time series of data, but rather the variance between the data of two time series.

The autocorrelation—also called serial correlation—can be defined, and computed, in the same way as correlation if, instead of considering two times series, we look at only one of them, and compute the correlation between a set of data of some size, and a set of same size but starting with a lag of 1 or several days before. If 1 day separates the two sets, the autocorrelation is said a "lag 1" autocorrelation; if 2 days separates them, a "lag 2" autocorrelation, etc. To the extent that if the autocorrelation is different from 0, it means that the value of a data of the time series is affected by the value of a previous day (−1 or minus x days).

As regards option pricing models, a first correlation problem, actually an autocorrelation problem, can happen as a partial breach to the randomness of time series of underlying prices. Probabilistic models like addressed in the "probabilistic models" subsection of Sect. 4.3 are built, among others, on the hypothesis that the random time series of underlying prices does not present any autocorrelation. Said in more formal terms, the corresponding returns must be IID ("Independently and Identically Distributed"): note that the condition of "Identically" excludes the non-stationarity. This is far from happening in the real life.

Practically speaking, to the extent that time series of returns present some autocorrelation, this will affect the volatility calculation. Intuitively, if the returns present some positive autocorrelation, the actual volatility (standard deviation) will be higher than the one computed in the traditional way, and conversely. And as regards the funds industry, we have the reverse relationship in the calculation of the key indicator called Sharpe ratio, since the volatility is in the denominator of this ratio.

Reminder 4.5: The Sharpe ratio

The Sharpe ratio is the usual performance measure, used in the portfolio management business. It presents the advantage of quantifying what should be the true meaning of the word "performance": even if, in the common language—included throughout this book—"performance" is used as a synonym of "return," a portfolio manager is supposed to deliver the highest possible return but also the lowest possible risk = volatility = standard deviation of returns. W. Sharpe combined these two features of a performance into his ratio, simply by—for a given reference period—dividing the obtained return by the associated risk. This must be slightly corrected because investing in riskless government bonds is obviously bringing no risk at all. So that in the formula it is the excess return *above the riskless return of a government paper (for a maturity equivalent to the reference period of the Sharpe ratio calculation) that must be divided by the risk.*

Note that the Sharpe ratio is not exempt of criticism, such as, by using the risk measure as a standard deviation, it does not take into account the possible skewness of the returns (cf. Sect. 5.1).

Andrew LO has proposed a formulation for taking into account k lags of autocorrelations ρ_k in the calculation of the annualized volatility σ, computed with a periodicity n, that is $\sigma\sqrt{n}$. It consists of replacing $\sqrt{n}$ by

$$n/\sqrt{n + 2\sum_{k=1}^{n-1}(n-k)\rho_k}$$

From the formula, we see that if a time series of returns presents autocorrelations of various lags that are globally negative, the actual per annual volatility is indeed higher, and conversely, with autocorrelations globally positive. But this relationship is of course only valid in absence of non-stationarity. Cf. Andrew LO, *The Statistics of Sharpe Ratios*, Financial Analysts Journal, Vol. 58, No 4, 2002, pp. 36–45.

- *options on baskets of assets*

Another correlation problem with option valuation concerns underlying baskets of assets. Option pricing models being first developed for a single underlying asset, say a stock, the question is how to adapt it when the underlying is a basket of several stocks. Let us first discard the very standard and liquid options on stock indexes, because the market practice considers a stock index as a single underlying, traded with its own market (implied) volatility. But in the case of any kind of bespoke baskets, pricing an option on them needs to compute a basket volatility, which involves the volatilities of each basket component as well as each correlation pair, weighted as in the basket.

So far, so good. But by doing so, we incorporate correlation coefficients which are hard to quantify. For two reasons which are linked to each other: on which past period of time to compute them, with enough accuracy? And what if there is some non-stationarity over such a period of time? There is no satisfying answer to that question, first because there is no (not yet?) satisfying probabilistic model for correlation. So that, once more, we are confronted with both an accuracy and a non-stationarity issues.

The volatility σ_B of a basket is the square root of its volatility

$$\sigma_B^2 = \sum_{i=1}^{N} w_i^2 \sigma_i^2 + 2\sum_{i=1}^{N}\sum_{j=1}^{N} w_i w_j \rho_{ij} \sigma_i \sigma_j$$

(notations are obvious). Now, as regards a probabilistic correlation model, there is unfortunately no stochastic process under the usual form of a differential equation. Researchers have developed techniques implementing *copulae*, that is, measures of co-dependence between two variates, which are independent of their individual marginal distributions (Cf., for example, Roger B. NELSEN, *An Introduction to Copulas*, Springer, 2010, 284 p.).

We face a similar problem of correlation between baskets of debt in securitization "tranches": yet, this correlation should be taken into consideration in the determination of the coupons of assets backed securities issued on these tranches, but hard to value in practice, for the reasons developed above. As an extreme case, the origin of the "sub-primes crisis" lies in this correlation feature.

Finally, we should also note that if the correlation is non-stationary, it is also necessarily the case for the "beta" measure, as currently used in portfolio management, since both measures are linked to each other.

Following the CAPM, regarding the relationship between the volatility of a stock σ_i and the volatility σ_M of the "market portfolio" or its stock index proxy, we have

$$\beta = \rho \frac{\sigma_i}{\sigma_M} \qquad \text{and} \qquad \rho = \frac{\sigma_{iM}}{\sigma_i \sigma_M}$$

where σ_{iM} is the covariance between i and M prices.

4.9 Algorithms: Quantitative ("Algorithmic") Trading Models

With respect to portfolio management, issues of data accuracy and of non-stationarity do actually also affect the building and the use of algorithms or quantitative trading models. It is for example the case of

- portfolio optimization techniques, such as "smart beta," which are affected by non-stationarity.

To illustrate this, let us take a multi-asset classes portfolio, initially invested ("long-only") in Euro STOXX 50, 10-year Bund, 10-year US T-bond, EUR/USD, Gold, and the commodity index CRB. This portfolio is equally weighted initially in each of these assets, from 01/01/2009. Let us look after its global (gross) performance after 4 years (until the end of 2012). We compare six different ways of rebalancing the portfolio, according to the following methodologies:

- "Buy (equally weighted) and hold" (not modifying the weights later on)
- Reset equal weighting at the beginning of each year
- At the end of each year, the next weightings resulting from a minimum variance criterion, practically, here, a minimum standard deviation criterion
- Conversely, at the end of each year, the next weightings resulting from a maximum variance criterion
- At the end of each year, the next weightings resulting from a minimum Sharpe ratio criterion
- At the end of each year, the next weightings resulting from a maximum Sharpe ratio criterion

After 4 years, the obtained performances were:

Weighting:	Risk	Rank	Return	Rank	Sharpe	Rank
Buy & hold:	13.25%	2	31.53%	4	2.82	3
Reset equ. w.:	14.88%	5	34.55%	3	2.76	4
Min vol:	15.74%	4	39.70%	1	3.01	2
Max vol:	5.47%	1	2.65%	6	0.38	6
Min Sharpe:	18.99%	6	18.96%	5	1.16	5
Max Sharpe:	14.71%	3	39.46%	2	3.20	1

Based on this example, it appears, over the 4 years, that:

- The best performance in risk is paradoxically reached with the maximum volatility criterion, followed by the buy and hold strategy. The best result can be explained by the "mean reverting" feature of the volatility, namely, waving over time from low volatility to high volatility regimes, and conversely. This may explain why—depending on the set of data! see below—having increased the weights of high volatility assets at the end of 1 year could benefit from a move back to lower volatility during the next year.

- The best performance in return, obtained with the minimum volatility criterion, can be explained in the same way (going next year to higher volatility can be profitable in a bullish market). The next best is given by the maximum Sharpe criterion (cf. below).

- Finally, as a combination of their respective rankings in risk and return separately, that is, by combining them both, in terms of return and in terms of risk, the best performance is unsurprisingly obtained by the maximum Sharpe criterion, followed by the minimum volatility criterion.

One should strongly emphasize that the output of this table will necessarily be different, if applied to another range of years, given the non-stationarity of the yearly performances. This example has been given only for illustration purpose. What we must draw as a conclusion is that, first, given, once more, the non-stationarity, it is unrealistic to hope finding an optimum between those criteria (or others, of the same kind), and, in particular, not trust upon the (although nicely) marketed "minimum variance" criterion.

Second, and more generally, in many similar optimization problems, the choice for a particular optimization criterion should have to be grounded in the conviction of the portfolio manager (based, for example, on fundamental analysis), who is, after all, paid for taking some risk, here in the choice of asset weights over time. In absence of any good reason/conviction to size the weights of each position over time, the only wise attitude should consist of a "neutral" attitude, starting equi-weighted and let it go (the first above criterion). This is as an application of the more general principle "if you cannot justify for a particular law to apply, keep neutral."

NB: By a pure coincidence, this approach has obtained the medium rank in the above table.

Continuing in the field of portfolio management, since the use of algorithms as quantitative trading models is growing, as an alternative to asset allocation grounded on fundamental analysis, it is worth to mention some other issues, related to the use of data:

- The crucial role of the size of the set of data used to build a quantitative trading model. Beyond the question of accuracy of resulting measures (volatility, etc.), because of the non-stationarity a model should be built and tested on two sub-periods of time which are big enough to cover enough different regimes of market behavior. This increases the chances to have built a robust model. If not, the model will not be robust enough, and may fail once applied during a market "regime" that had not been incorporated in the building of the model.

- The impact, crucial as well, of the differences between collected data (close prices or any others) from usual databases, and real trading conditions ("slippage"). At least, the model should take into account a realistic margin, wider than market bid–ask spreads, on used data prices.

- The *obsolescence* risk: markets behaviors are changing over time for so many reasons, just two examples: the huge volumes traded today by ETF funds, and the impact of high-frequency trading. So that a model could have been adequately adapted on past data, but become obsolete after a couple of years.

- Not taking care of the causality principle is a latent risk. That is, the risk, for a model, to erroneously using some data set to explain the behavior of other data. In some situations, this may be viewed as a variety of obsolescence risk, that is, if some causality link has existed earlier, but any more later on, due to markets changes of behavior.

- Using moving averages or moving regressions (although less frequent) as trend-following indicators in building a quantitative trading model is also subject to non-stationarity. All the more, due to a key parameter of such calculations, that is to say, the "window" (i.e., number) of data used in the calculation. These tools are said "lagging" indicators, depending on the use of more or less past data.

A too-small window would probably less suffer from a non-stationarity but lead to excessively "noisy" results, while a too long window will, first, give rise to an excessively late signal, but also be more affected by changes of market "regime." Despite the lagging effect, users of these indicators are considering them as predictive tools: this would be the case in a stationary world, but in social sciences and in particular financial markets, this is not the case!

- By not enough taking into account the above points, as it is so frequent to observe in the real life, the "blank" performance of a quantitative trading model will not be confirmed once actually implemented in the market or less and less confirmed (obsolescence). Moreover, in the case of a portfolio manager is using a quantitative model built from some outside supplier, he will not have access to the core of the model, as a black box, and therefore have no way to make sure enough such model has been developed in a safe way.

4.10 As a Conclusion to This Chapter: Issues About Modeling

Any model being subject to various kind of approximations of the reality, subject to some degree of shortcoming, G. Box and N. Draper[3] are well—even somewhat provocatively—summarizing the situation by saying "Remember that all models are wrong; the practical question is how wrong do they have to be to not be useful."

For the readers interested to go deeper about modeling, Jarrow's paper cited in the footnote about Box and Draper provides a nice analysis (despite its title, it is actually not limited to risk management models), starting with a taxonomy of models—statistical and theoretical—then distinguishing between robust and non-robust assumptions ("hypotheses," as called in the present book), testing models, estimation of a theoretical model's parameters, calibration, etc., with many examples of usual probabilistic models, qualified as "erroneous" or not, and concluding by a "How to properly use a model" section.

[3]Box and Draper, *Empirical model-building and response surfaces*, Wiley, 1987. Cited by Robert Jarrow in *Risk management models: construction, testing, usage*, Johnson School Research Paper Series No. 38-2010.

Chapter 5
Financial Data: Some Risk Management Issues

Issues about data and their models inevitably concern risk management activities, in portfolio management, fund management, and more generally, in all activities linked to the use of financial data. As regards issues about models, it is not surprising that financial regulators include the model risk in their regulations about risk management, this type of risk being included in the category of "operational risk," to avoid creating a particular entry, besides main entries such as market risk, liquidity risk, etc.

5.1 Using the Volatility Measure of Losses, That Is, of Negative Returns

Risk managers as well as regulators are using the standard deviation (volatility) measure in almost all of their calculation, the underlying distribution (let us say, in returns) being Gaussian, or skewed. To the extent that the real distributions are not Gaussian, to a more or less extent, and given risk is focusing on losses, the use of the standard deviation (volatility) of losses, that is, of negative returns, would be preferable for risk management purpose. It would constitute a way to cope with the degree of skewness of the returns.

In particular, it is worth noticing that there are very few reports of fund management companies disclosing the Sortino ratio of their funds, i.e., the equivalent of the Sharpe ratio but based on this standard deviation of negative returns. Furthermore, a monitoring of the standard deviation of negative returns would be useful, for example, under the form of the ratio of the standard deviation of negative returns by the standard deviation of positive returns, or alternatively, by the global standard deviation.

A. Ruttiens, *Decision Making with Quantitative Financial Market Data*,
SpringerBriefs in Operations Research,
https://doi.org/10.1007/978-3-030-67580-6_5

Denoting σ_d and σ_u the downside (on negative returns) and upside (on positive returns) semi-standard deviations, respectively, one should not have to be surprised that they both are $<\sigma$, given their application range is more or less twice narrower than the one of σ, with $\sigma_d + \sigma_u > \sigma$.

5.2 The Time's Arrow Matters: The "Accrued Returns Variability" Measure

Usual statistics ignore the time's arrow: measures such as average, standard deviation, skewness, etc., are computed from data series processed as if they were concomitant. But what if these statistics are applied on financial "*time*" series of data? To illustrate this observation, let us start with the following example: consider the two following time series, #1 and #2, representing the 251 successive daily Net Asset Values of two (portfolios or) funds over a 1-year period.

To facilitate the comparison, both have been scaled so that their initial NAV = 100. At the end of the year, both funds NAV reached the same level, of about 145, so that they have achieved the same performance of about +45%. But their performance has evolved quite differently during the year:

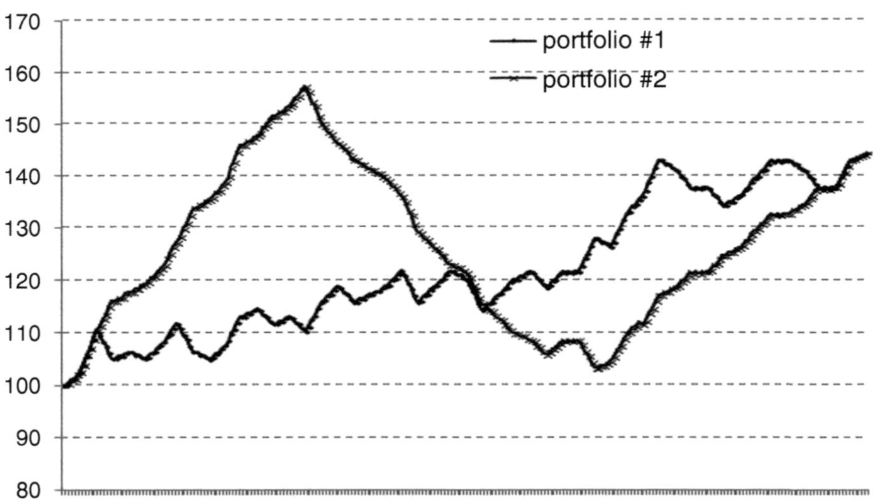

From an investor's viewpoint, after 1-year fund #2 looks significantly more risky, given more prices dispersion during the course of the year. She will not need calculations to be convinced that the volatility of fund #2 is higher. Even if at the end of the year they both present the same achieved performance, fund #1 should be preferred by more risk averse investors. Unfortunately, these two (fictitious) funds and performances were built so that both prices (or share values) series present the same starting point ($100), the same ending point ($144.28), *but also* the same returns average, same variance and volatility or standard deviation, as well as same skewness and kurtosis.

To do that, we have simply arranged the same set of returns for both time series in a different order. Their annualized volatility is 9.91% each. Such equal volatility measure is therefore not reflecting the higher dispersion (in its original sense) of performances actually showed by fund #2, versus the smaller one of fund #1. So that, besides the volatility measure, we should need a quantitative measure that translates the qualitative measure of this "dispersion," not incorporated into the volatility measure.

By the way, if such a measure would help the investor (or potential investor) to take into account the situation presented above, we should also point out that, for its asset manager, confronted with risk management constraints, fund #2 is probably more difficult to manage properly than fund #1, despite they present the same volatility: indeed, during the extensive deteriorating phase of his performance, asset manager #2 will most probably have been encouraged (by himself, or his top management, or due to risk management constraints) to modify his exposure, what is not the case with asset manager #1.

This example shows that for statistics applied on non-concomitant data, the time's arrow matters. So that, to go further in the rationale of what should actually be a suitable risk measure toward a riskless investment, one should incorporate the impact of the time's arrow in it. This can be achieved by not restricting the "riskless" notion to the absence of volatility (standard deviation) of successive performances, but by extending this notion to *how* the riskiness is actually rewarded to the investor, that is, by producing a progressive *accrued* revenue, in conformity with the Mark-to-Market and IFRS accounting practices.

This leads us to introduce a dispersion measure, under the name of "ARV," for "accrued returns variability".[1]

Some more about ARV:

To translate the objective of producing a risk measure that incorporates the impact of the passage of time, it suffices to compute, at each successive (daily, weekly or monthly) time interval, the spread between the risky, actual *cumulated* intermediate returns, and the corresponding ones, obtained at the end of the observations period if the resulting global return were equally accrued over the successive time intervals. Then, a suitable risk measure can be computed by handling the series of these successive spreads in the same way as a series of successive individual returns.

The ARV can thus be defined as the standard deviation of a series of spreads between the successive *cumulated* returns, and the corresponding successive equally accrued revenues totalizing the return achieved on the whole period. The graph below is showing this spread on day 7 for fund #1, and separately on day 8 for fund #2 (spreads on the same day would appear less clearly on the graph):

[1]This market risk measure has been deliberately named a "variability" measure, to avoid confusion with the "volatility" measure.

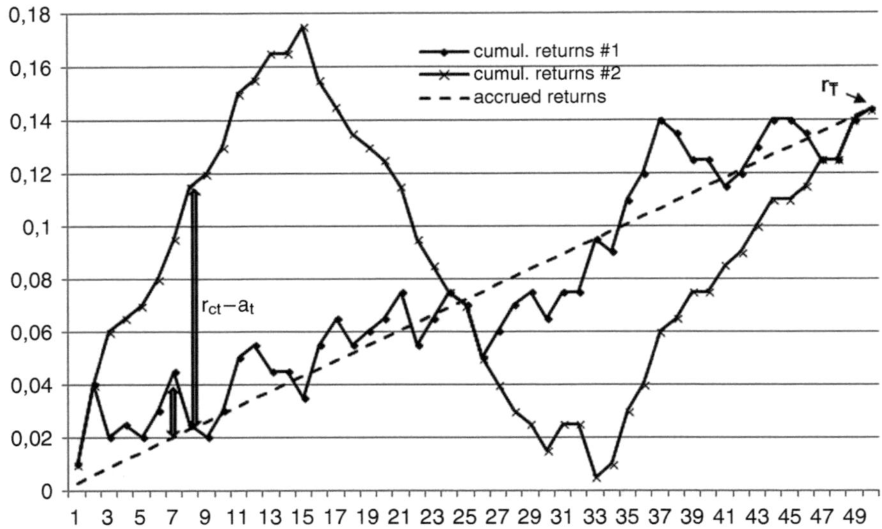

For a risk measure relative to a series of returns r_j, ($j = 1,\ldots,n$), over a past period T, computed on n equal subperiods of time Δt ($\Delta t = 1$ day for example) such as $n\Delta t = T$, with $c_{j\Delta t}$ being the cumulated return achieved on the jth sub-period, $a_{j\Delta t}$ the equally *accrued* return from $t = 0$ to $j\Delta t$, m the average of the $\{c_{j\Delta t} - a_{j\Delta t}\}$ series of spreads, and r_T the return achieved on the whole period T,

$$\mathrm{ARV} = \sqrt{\frac{1}{n}\sum_{j=1}^{n}\left[\left(c_{j\Delta t} - a_{j\Delta t}\right) - m\right]^2}$$

with

$$a_{j\Delta t} = \frac{j}{n} r_T \qquad j = 1, \ldots, n$$

Coming back to the investor or portfolio manager confronted with any invested asset, the more performance is achieved in a steady way over time, the surer it is, being a positive or a negative performance: the investor is entitled to grant more trust to the underlying investment policy, and—as far as the performance is positive—the portfolio manager is less forced to portfolio adjustments.

To summarize, the ARV is nothing more than a risk measure, but more representative of the risk in the sense of the amplitude of performance fluctuations, than the traditional volatility, because it takes into account the time's arrow. By the way, among the various usual risk measures, the only one also taking into account of the time's arrow is the Maximum Draw Down measure, discussed in Sect. 5.3.

For more information about the ARV, including its application to real funds performances, Cf. Alain Ruttiens, *Portfolio Risk Measures: The Time's Arrow Matters*, Journal of Computational Economics, March 2013.

5.3 The Case of the Controversial VaR ("Value at Risk") Measure

Reminder 5.1: The VaR measure of risk

The VaR is a risk measure, as being the estimated possible loss, expressed as an amount of $ (or any other currency), that a single position or a whole portfolio in financial instruments can suffer, over a given horizon of time, with respect to some given probability level, called the confidence level. *In short, the VaR is a measure of market (downside) risk on an aggregated (portfolio) level. VaR and conditional VaR (cf. below) are commonly used for quantifying a risk of loss and may be required by market regulators in the banks as well in the funds industry sectors.*

A basic example:

Consider a portfolio having as a sole position $100M invested in the SP500. Based on a series of past data of daily SP500 close prices and corresponding returns, one can draw the histogram of these daily returns:

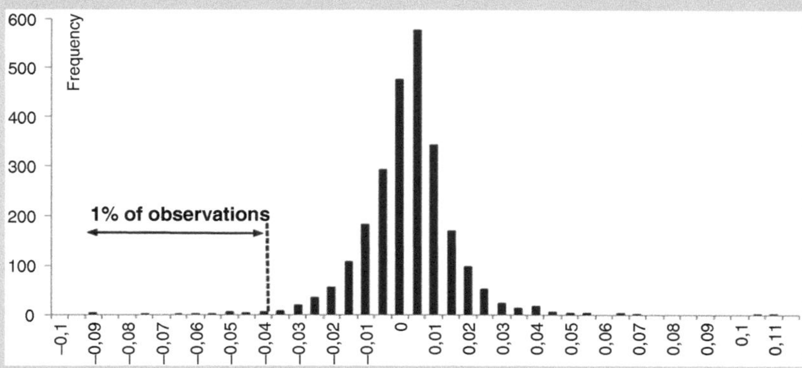

Question: How much this fund is likely to lose on the next day (or during a defined longer period of time), with a probability of 1%? The answer is: a 1-day VaR at a 99% confidence level, that is, the cumulated losses, up to 1%, called the corresponding "significance level." On the graph, it corresponds to a loss of −4%, hence the VaR of this portfolio is $100M × 0.04 = $4M: this portfolio has 1% chances to lose −4% in 1 day. It does not mean that is its maximum possible loss: indeed, according to the graph, the loss can exceed −4%, but with a probability of less than 1%.

The VaR parameters:

- *Confidence level "c": the higher the* c, *the higher the VaR. Indeed, continuing with the example, 1% chance of loss, i.e.,* c *= 99% with a VaR of $4M is more severe than 5% chance of loss (*c *= 95%), with a*

(continued)

Reminder 5.1 (continued)

corresponding VaR of ≈$2.25% (moving the marker to the right, on the above graph).

– *Period of time: the VaR amount increases with the period of time it refers to, because the loss at risk is understandably higher over a longer period. A VaR on a 20-days period is higher than on a 1 day. (NB: The VaR on a 20-days period is the standard for UCITS funds regulations).*

A variant of the VaR: the Conditional VaR, or C-VaR, or "Expected shortfall," aiming to size the average loss beyond the corresponding VaR level (left side on the graph). Zooming the tail of the histogram:

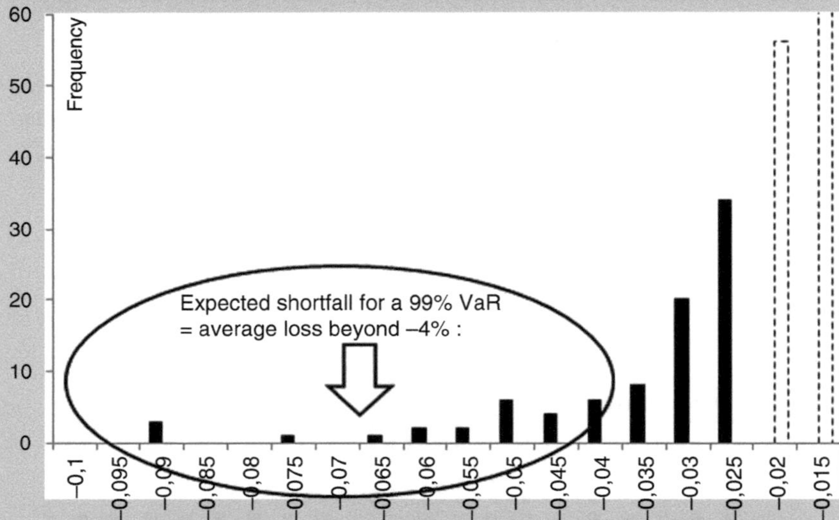

This section addresses the problem raised with (very) low probability measures (tails), already mentioned at the end of Chap. 1, and also in Sect. 4.5 about credit derivatives. VaR measures are obviously confronted with this problem.

To introduce the subject, let us first compare two extreme cases of probability calculations:

– The case of a lottery with 1 million tickets and one single prize: the probability to win is 10^{-6}.

– The case of the incidence of a major earthquake ($M \geq 7.0$) in the Paris area within the next 50 years: the probability of such an incidence has been computed as 0.02% before 2050.[2]

In the first case, the probability determination is obviously 100% accurate. In the second case, the earthquake probability of 0.0002 is valid to the extent of the accuracy of its calculation methodology, and subject to a sampling size issue (i.e., the set of relevant historical data), that is: quality and quantity of the input data, type of probability distribution (Gaussian or others), and, of course, (non-)stationarity.

Inaccuracies also arise from the various methodologies used for a VaR computation. By the way, several studies have evidenced that different methodologies applied to a common portfolio significantly lead to different results.

To analyze the three main methodologies:

- The "variance–covariance" method is obviously subject to the weakness of the hypothesis of a Gaussian distribution, and to the non-stationarity of the variances, covariances, or correlations used in the calculation (cf. end of Chap. 4).
- The "historical method" presents the advantage of not imposing a (Gaussian) distribution, but is much depending on the size of data base, and, because of a risk of non-stationarity, to the validity of its ex-post application.
- The Monte Carlo simulations method is of course affected by a model risk (Cf. Sect. 4.6).

And moreover, at the level of the whole portfolio, all of the three methods are affected by the hypothesis of considering pair correlations as constant.

Finally, given a VaR calculation being performed on each of the assets of a portfolio, then aggregated into a single value for the whole portfolio, needless to say, that this aggregation involves the use of correlation pairs, which are varying with time, i.e., the horizon of time needed to collect enough data for individual VaR calculations. Once more, the problem of squaring the circle (cf. end of Chap. 3).

VaR measures being linked to a low percentage of cumulated probabilities, it is well established that they are all the more sensitive to the above issues. As said earlier, probability distributions and related statistics are uncomfortable with rare events.

It should be noted in passing that a way to significantly reduce such errors in the VaR calculation would consist, instead of computing the VaR "ingredients" on the positions in a portfolio, in computing it on a series of past performances of the portfolio itself. Of course, this would not bypass all of the error sources, but at least the ones linked to correlations. And the non-stationarity of asset prices is replaced here by the one of the portfolio management style over time. But this would make sense for a portfolio management style that is deliberately more or less kept consistent over time. To the author's knowledge, this approach is not accepted by regulators (because of this question of possible changes in the portfolio management); however, this kind of VaR calculation is practiced by some management companies, for internal use.

[2] Source: TX Earthquake report, Texas (USA).

Now, besides usual criticisms about the VaR, we will go a step further, which starts with a fundamental question: Is it reasonable to include a probability measure in a calculation that must lead to a decision—in this context, about risk management—or that will affect a decision? To be affirmative, the answer to this question must necessarily involve a sufficient degree of *pertinence* of the measure involved in the calculation, in other words, that this measure satisfactorily represents the reality or the reliability of the phenomenon which has been quantified in the measure.

If it is not the case, it makes sense that the use of such a probability measure would better be restricted to a stylized fact, that is, to its actual equivalent of a qualitative assessment (somewhere between "very low probability" and "highly probable"). So that the previous question can be reformulated as: To what extent a probability measure should be valid enough to be safely used in a quantitative way, within the framework of a decision process? And the answer is: It depends on its degree of *pertinence*.

The paper of Adela BAHO and Alain RUTTIENS (*Probability and Pertinence*, Risk Management eJournal, Vol. 6, N° 128, Dec 15, 2014 and also in International Journal of Business and Management Study, vol. 2, issue 1, 2014) is proposing an objective, quantitative measure, called "π," of the degree of pertinence of a probability metrics. So that the pertinence π, associated with a given probability percentage, reflects the precision of this percentage through its link to the confidence interval which is associated to. This allows to assess the degree of pertinence of a probability measure that would be involved in any kind of calculation leading to a risk management decision.

Altogether, before incorporating a probability measure into her decision process, a decision-maker would do well to take into account the degree of pertinence π of this probability, and possibly give up to make use of this probability measure in her calculations if its pertinence π is judged too small, i.e., below some minimum threshold. Alternatively, facing (very) low probabilities, instead of dealing with (very) low probability measures, characterized by a (too) low pertinence level, a decision-maker should rather incorporate it into her decision-making process on a qualitative rather than on a quantitative basis.

As an example, in an interview (LE POINT, 17/10/13), professor Didier Sicard, past president of the French *Comité Consultatif National d'Ethique*, declared "To know that you have 2.1% chances more than your neighbor to develop such or such disease is a derisory negligible information" (translated from French), showing an intuitive perception of our pertinence issue.

Coming back to the VaR, in Sect. 3.1 we have introduced the confidence interval measure, saying, among others that "This confidence interval, and corresponding accuracy, is mainly depending on the size of the data used for their calculation," and showed how the confidence interval may be computed on an "ex-post" basis (i.e., a series of past data), for a given error and sample size.

But, logically, if we recognize the importance of the sample size to determine with enough accuracy a VaR value, we should keep the same care once we look after its actual application in the next, say 1 day or 20 days, i.e., on an "ex ante" basis as well. Once the probability (for example, 1%, with a 99% VaR) of a certain VaR amount of loss has been computed with some accepted error margin, in order to observe the occurrence of the event with this 1% probability, one should look after it on a sample of the same size (n) or number of days to come, if we want to observe the possible loss with the same error margin. A smaller sample size of some days to come will not reflect this probability of occurrence. This is the heart of the problem with the VaR application. Strangely enough, up to now, researchers had worked a lot on the accuracy of a VaR calculation, but not on the validity of its application afterward.

As an example, let us consider the 99% VaR calculation on a given fund, to be applied on the next 100 days, with a margin error of 10% around the 1% confidence level of this VaR. Because of this short sample size of 100 days, the VaR loss, supposed to occur with a 1% chance, may actually occur with a probability ranging from 0% chances up to 2.28%! (for details of the calculation, cf. the above-mentioned paper). Because a 100-days period would not be realistic, since the portfolio composition will most probably have changed meanwhile, the ESMA regulator imposes a norm on the 99% VaR for the next month (20 business days) instead, but this leads to an even larger probability range of VaR loss occurrence. This is not compatible with the spirit, nor with the objective of the VaR as a risk measure: the VaR is not a pertinent measure.

A way to make it more pertinent would consist in strongly reducing the confidence level of the VaR: instead of 99% as required for example in the ESMA regulation, why not going down to the range of 90 $\rightarrow$ 70%? Of course, since in this range of values, the VaR amount of loss would be significantly lower, the VaR limit enforced by the regulator should be adjusted accordingly. As a matter of fact, in the case of the ESMA regulation for UCITS funds, for example, requiring a 99% VaR of a maximum of 20% of the NAV of a fund, the authorized maximum should be much lower.

Assuming a Gaussian distribution of returns, it would be easy to compute an "implied" VaR limit at some lower confidence level, equivalent to the 20% maximum of the NAV for a 99% VaR.

Furthermore, as regards conditional VaR (Expected Shortfall) measure, dealing with a range of even lower probabilities than for the VaR, and because of the difficulty to collect enough, and accurate, data covering the left extremity of the probability distribution, a credible, pertinent enough, calculation is just a dream.

- an alternative "Risk at Value" measure

Besides the above criticism of the VaR measure, while recognizing its use as a fact in risk management regulations and practices, we have to emphasize the inappropriateness of the VaR concept, when applied in the funds industry. Regulators have indeed "copy-pasted" to the funds industry the principle of VaR regulation earlier imposed in the banks sector. To summarize, the VaR aims to compute some expected, potential loss, for a given probability level. In the case of funds management, this makes much less sense than the opposite, that is, answering the question "At which probability level could I suffer a given loss amount?". For example, if, as a fund/portfolio manager, I would like as much as possible to avoid suffering a loss of let us say 18% of my NAV, my concern is to determine what is the probability that this loss would occur, within the next x days. The choice of a threshold (18% in the above example) is of course somewhat arbitrary, but one could for example use the MDD (maximum Draw Down) suffered on some past history of the fund, given the prominence of this measure by market practitioners.

The answer to this question amounts to compute a VaR backward—hence, the proposed name of "Risk at Value" (RaV)—with the same way of modus operandi and, however, with the same inaccuracy. But while we are at it, computing a RaV would be a more rational approach than computing a VaR, with respect to funds risk management.

Chapter 6
Synthesis

Everybody involved with the use of financial data should be concerned with:

- The degree of accuracy of these data, determined in an adequate way.
- The degree of non-stationarity of the probability distributions of the data time series used for computing measures, such as average, volatility, correlation, etc.
- The validity and the reliability of pricing tools, risk management tools, software, and more generally any kind of quantitative models working on these data. Not only because of inherent accuracy and stationarity problems, and the associated problem of "squaring the circle," but also because of:
  - Simplifying assumptions (the hypotheses of the model),
  - The rationale of the underlying model approach,

all of these issues as developed in the previous chapters of this book. This concern would all the more apply to people in charge of building in-house software and quantitative models making use of said data.

By the way, not only financial modelers but everybody concerned with data treatment would be wise to keep in mind, and apply, some of the commitments of the "Hippocratic oath" of E. Derman and P. Wilmott in their *Financial Modelers' Manifesto*, namely:

> ~ *Though I will use models boldly to estimate value, I will not be overly impressed by mathematics.*
> ~ *I will never sacrifice reality for elegance without explaining why I have done so.*
> ~ *Nor will I give the people who use my model false comfort about its accuracy. Instead, I will make explicit its assumptions and oversights.*

A. Ruttiens, *Decision Making with Quantitative Financial Market Data*,
SpringerBriefs in Operations Research,
https://doi.org/10.1007/978-3-030-67580-6_6

MIX
Papier aus verantwortungsvollen Quellen
Paper from responsible sources
FSC® C105338

If you have any concerns about our products,
you can contact us on
ProductSafety@springernature.com

In case Publisher is established outside the EU,
the EU authorized representative is:
Springer Nature Customer Service Center GmbH
Europaplatz 3, 69115 Heidelberg, Germany

Printed by Libri Plureos GmbH
in Hamburg, Germany